Riding the Wind

A Test Pilot's Story

Riding the Wind

A Test Pilot's Story

Wg Cdr P Ashoka, VM & Bar

(Established 1870)

Centre for Armed Forces Historical Research

United Service Institution of India

New Delhi

Vij Books India Pvt Ltd

New Delhi (India)

Published by

Vij Books India Pvt Ltd
(Publishers, Distributors & Importers)
2/19, Ansari Road
Delhi – 110 002
Phones: 91-11-43596460, 91-11-47340674
Fax: 91-11-47340674
e-mail: vijbooks@rediffmail.com

Copyright © 2019, United Service Institution of India, New Delhi

ISBN: 978-93-88161-64-0 (Hardback)
ISBN: 978-93-88161-65-7 (ebook)

All rights reserved.

No part of this book may be reproduced, stored in a retrieval system, transmitted or utilised in any form or by any means, electronic, mechanical, photocopying, recording or otherwise, without the prior permission of the copyright owner. Application for such permission should be addressed to the publisher.

In fond memory of

My elder brother, Wg Cdr P Gautam, MVC and Bar, VM

My younger brother, Wg Cdr P Ajit, VM

Contents

Foreword	ix
Preface	xiii
Types of Aircraft Flown by the Author	xiv
Acknowledgements	xv
1. Call of the Armed Forces	1
2. Learning to Fly	3
3. The First Jet Fighter of the IAF	12
4. The First Transonic Jet Fighter of the IAF	23
5. The Smallest Transonic Jet Fighter	36
6. Test Pilot Training	43
7. Early Years as a Test Pilot	58
8. Aircraft and Armament Testing Unit	67
9. Test Flying Transport Aircraft and Gliders	79
10. Supersonics	98
11. Hindustan Aeronautics Ltd Bangalore Part I	129
12. Hindustan Aeronautics Ltd Bangalore Part II	156
13. Test Flying Light Aircraft	169
My Brother Wg. Cdr. P. Gautam, MVC and bar, VM	179
The Family	181

Foreword

Wg Cdr Padmanabha Ashoka, VM and Bar, joined the Indian Airforce as a fighter pilot on 16th January 1954. A mere three days earlier I turned five—quite unaware at that time that our lives were destined to intersect some two decades later. By the time we first met at HAL Nasik Division, he already was an accomplished test pilot respected by the entire test flying fraternity. His reputation used to precede him as by then he had become the go-to professional for test flights that were out of the ordinary. Such flights needed to be done nonetheless for critical operational reasons.

In this book, he shares technical details with the reader while using uncomplicated, easy to understand language. While providing explanations regarding inherent challenges faced by test pilots, he has also explained complex aerodynamic concepts without robbing the narrative of either the excitement or the risks involved while performing rarely flown test flights.

Having observed him from up close while I was a rookie test pilot, but also privileged to have been his protégé at HAL Nasik Division in the late '70s, I can say without any doubt that he has been overly modest in recounting his various exploits. For example, quite simply stated, he was the `Master of the skies' when at the controls of the Mig 21 aircraft. The aircraft seemed to be a mere extension of him while he performed what appeared to the uninitiated, hair raising manoeuvres. As for those in the know, it was always a flawless demonstration of precision, excellence and beauty. There was a lot to learn and I did just that, by merely observing his analytical approach to problem-solving, even when problems observed during test flights seemed intractable.

In this book, we have been provided a rare first-person insight into the way operational pilots are 'blooded' during test pilot's courses, specially the one he attended at the Empire Test Pilot`s school at Farnborough, UK.

It was an experience that shaped his professional outlook. I noticed that he employed a similar methodology while mentoring his juniors, myself included. He believed in empowering inexperienced test pilots by encouraging them to think things through themselves. This included an examination of all 'what ifs' before arriving at a professional decision. This was his way of preparing junior test pilots to operate independently, as that precisely would be the lonely landscape they would be operating in during their careers. He challenged us to be worthy of the trust reposed in us both by him and our specialisation and, more often than not, I suspect we came up to his expectations.

Another aspect of his mentorship was his steadfast support to his team members when they came under subtle pressures to dilute somewhat, standards of aircraft acceptance. This support was hugely comforting. It resulted in the re-inforcement of the unwritten code of test flying: the test pilot is honour bound to report and draw conclusions from what he observes in flight, compare that observation with acceptance criteria, and not what he infers, interprets, or later, rationalises before pronouncing judgement on the acceptance of an aircraft, or the performance of one of its systems.

This book caters to diverse audiences. Civilian readership will gain an insight into the world of test flying, while the professional reader receives gems of experimentally derived wisdom that Wg. Cdr. Ashoka gained during his remarkably challenging professional career. That said, I feel that a test pilot and professional of his calibre, ability and potential, was born a bit too early from the standpoint of our country's Aircraft Development Industry. Or stated differently, the calendar gap that existed between the HF-24 'Marut' and Tejas Fighter development programme, resulted in his experience and skills remaining largely under-utilised during that period.

Irrespective of their fields of endeavour, those who become legends in their own lifetimes, are known not to shy away from revealing their own mistakes and their insecurities. As expected, the reader has been made privy to some of these anecdotal details as well.

To underline only the professional exploits of P Ashoka, would be to describe only half the man. It is my belief that a good professional becomes a great professional only when, in addition to one's core professional skills, one is also blessed by a keen sense of observation, a sensitive nature and genuine empathy towards other human beings. By that token,

Foreword

he is a truly great professional - one who has dedicated five long decades of his lifetime to military aviation while testing cutting edge technologies.

His professional life and achievements would have gained him a much deserved entry into the Indian Test Pilots' Hall of Fame. Pity, the country does not have one.

It is now left to us to Salute this Test Pilot Extraordinaire.

Wg Cdr Rakesh Sharma (Retd)

Ashoka Chakra
Research Cosmonaut
India
28 Jul 2018

Preface

When I retired in 2002 after completing 8000 hours of active flying over a period of 50 years, I had no inkling that I would end up writing a book on it. But some suggestions from my family and friends made me think over the possibility. I realised that by virtue of my unusually long innings in test flying, I had the privilege of having been through many unique experiences in the air, which if not duly recorded, would inevitably pass away into oblivion. It saddened me to think that such a fate awaits my demise. So, I sat down with paper and pen, wondering if I would be able to recall events stretching over 50 long gone years! But the human mind has often some magic up its sleeves, and as I scratched my head to dig deep into the past, graphic details of my flying experiences came surging forth, and each bit felt as if it had occurred just the other day! From there on, it was an effortless stroll, and I was able to relate with great accuracy what all I had been through in the air. So, here it is, in all stark detail.

I can only hope that the reader may find it at least somewhat interesting, if nothing else.

Types of Aircraft Flown by the Author

Tigermoth, HT-2, Harvard, Chipmunk, Piston Provost, Auster Otter, Krishak, Revathi, Basant, Rutan Long-easy, HPT-32, HTT-34, PC-9, Optica, Swati, Motor Glider, Hansa, Kiran Mk.1, Kiran Mk.2, Jet Provost, Bell G-2, Chetak, Cheetah, Devon, Dakota, Heron, Ilyushin-14, Nord-262, Skyvan, C-119 Packet, Caribou, Constellation, Viscount, BAC 1-11, VC-10, HS-748, Dornier-228, Comet-2E, Islander, Canberra, Vampire, Toofani, Mystere 4, Gnat Mk.1, Ajeet, Ajeet trainer, Hunter, Scimitar, Meteor-7, Meteor-8, Lightning 4, HF-24, MIG-21, Mig-23, Mig-27, Mig-29, Mirage-2000, Jaguar.

Acknowledgements

My grateful thanks to:

1. Squadron Leader Rana TS Chhina of Center for Armed Forces Historical Research/ United Service Institution of India for doing me the honour of accepting my book for publication and providing advice and support throughout the project. A special thanks to AVM Vikram Singh for his hugely supportive interest in the book, and for the inspiring concept of the cover design.

2. My daughter-in-law, Priti, for her encouragement, deep interest, and relentless efforts towards editing the script, and for scouting for publishers.

3. Dr. MS Rajamurthy, for so generously typing out the entire handwritten script, and for his tireless efforts in preparing and finalising the photographs for inclusion in the book. Also for his ever-ready assistance in any matter related to progress of the book.

4. Wg Cdr Rakesh Sharma, for his very generous and incisive foreword, and for his abiding friendship.

5. My wife Meera, my daughter Vrinda, and my son Dileep, for their silent support, patience and forbearance during the long decades of my obsessive involvement with flying.

Call of the Armed Forces

When I was in college in 1949, I had applied to join the Army. It was a timely telegram from my older brother Gautam, who was already at the Joint Services Wing of National Defence Academy (NDA), as an Airforce cadet, that led me to eventually join the Airforce rather than the Army!

Gautam had sent an urgent telegram to my parents in Indore, strongly advising against my joining the Army, and to apply for the IAF instead. The telegram arrived when I was already enroute to Mysore for the Army selection and had stopped for a day in Poona to meet my cousin. Visit over, I had boarded the train to Bangalore when my cousin's husband rushed into my compartment and said, "Gautam has sent a telegram. You have to get off." I had no time to argue with him as the whistle had blown and the train was beginning to move. I grabbed my things and jumped off.

Gautam was already an IAF cadet in January 1950. His term in JSW had given him a taste of army life and he was thoroughly disenchanted with it. He felt that the IAF, with its accent on flying, would be a better life. And so his telegram urging me to do the same.

I cancelled my visit to the Army Selection Board at Mysore and applied for joining JSW as an IAF cadet. In due course, I was selected for No. 4 course at JSW, Clement town, Dehradun, which I joined in June 1950.

At JSW, we had a tough and challenging two years of training. Our days were chock full with activity: classes in science and arts, PT, drill, games, boxing, riding, swimming, camping, long distance running, night treks in the wooded hills, and to top it all, strict inspections, often leading to punishments for slip-ups. It toughened us up right and proper. I felt a great sense of achievement when I completed the training successfully and passed out in June 1952. A few months later, I reported to the IAF Academy, Begumpet at Secunderabad, to start my flying career as a flight cadet.

Learning to Fly

Tiger Moth & Harvard

The time when one starts to learn flying holds a special place in every pilot's heart. The moment I started flying, I was fascinated by it. Now, after completing decades of military flying of complex machines, when I look back on it all, the initial bit of flying training which launched me into this dream world appears like a fairy tale.

We were a full 150 flight cadets when we started our flying training in September 1952 in Begumpet, Secunderabad. Only 46 succeeded in getting their 'wings' – the rest were mostly eliminated prior to going solo on the Tiger Moth. The only aim in life at that time was to go solo; little else mattered.

Tiger Moth

As machines go, the Tiger Moth was sweetness itself. It had none of the menacing looks that some other machines have. Its twin moth-wings were made of yellow fabric, and the softly purring propeller gave it a friendly pastoral personality, much to the relief of the young pupil pilot. The most delightful thing about the Tiger Moth was the open cockpit, giving you a real feel of being in the air. One had, of course, to use those large British goggles over the leather helmet. But there was no radio or proper intercom, and the instructor had to talk through a primitive contraption, somewhat like a long pipe with a funnel.

The aircraft had a small piston engine with a two-bladed wooden propeller. The fuel tank was located above the pilot's head in the middle of the top wing. A transparent panel on the tank enabled the pilot to visually check the fuel level, there being no fuel content gauge. For some unknown reason, the designer had not provided it with a tail wheel. Instead, there was a tail *skid*, which dragged on the ground during taxiing. The very first challenge to my reaction time and alertness presented itself during the procedure for starting the engine. The propeller had to be hand cranked by a mechanic with one magneto switch on, and the second magneto had to be switched on the moment the engine fired, and no earlier, to ensure safety of the mechanic. This was of course easier said than done, as it required a split second reaction.

A failed start would inevitably bring on an unpleasant outburst from the instructor. But practice and familiarity can, over time, change a seemingly difficult task to one of sure habit. And soon enough, I had no problem with it.

The Tiger Moth did not have any brakes for taxying on ground, and while it could be turned to the left or right by application of rudder, bringing it to a dead stop was a completely passive affair. One had to throttle back the engine to idle and wait for the rubbing of the tail skid on the ground to produce the desired result. This sometimes took quite some distance, especially if you had a tail wind or the ground was sloping. The result was a few scary moments, till I realized that the only solution was to anticipate and to be one step ahead of the aircraft- a very valuable lesson for the future. Probably the single biggest sin I ever committed then was to not keep the slip-skid ball in the centre during turns. This meant that the aircraft would skid and not be balanced, and much of the dressing down I got from my instructor was on this account. It was only much later that I came to appreciate how that unwanted sideways skid could ruin your gunnery scores!

Bit by bit I learnt to fly this beautiful aeroplane well enough to go solo. One day, after a few landings, my instructor parked the aircraft on the shoulder of the runway, came over to my cockpit and said, "It's all yours now." No words can ever describe what I felt at that moment; as if all my life's ambitions had been suddenly granted.

The fresh responsibility could have been overwhelming, had the challenge been less tantalizing. There was no time to think of anything other than the task at hand, and all my faculties had to focus on that and that alone. How many times in the future, in different circumstances and different cockpits, often with danger staring me in the face, the same scenario would play out and I would need to keep a relatively cool head and to only think of what had to be done.

I went over my cockpit checks slowly and twice over, then taxied on to the runway for takeoff. I opened throttle gradually and fully, keeping the aircraft straight with the help of rudders. After a while, I pushed the stick firmly forward and the tail came up enabling a grand view of the runway ahead over the vacant front cockpit. As the aircraft gained flying speed, I eased the stick back gently and was airborne. Hurrah! I was now a pilot on my first solo flight.

I climbed to 3,000 feet and carried out the gentle manoeuvres I was briefed on. The horizon was crystal clear and the numerous ponds and lakes around the airfield sparkled like jewels in the distance. The engine droned at a constant reassuring pitch and the control stick felt like a magic wand with which I could perform miracles. Turning the Tiger Moth required the pilot to get one of the cross wires that were fixed between the top and bottom wings parallel to the horizon, thus giving him the correct bank angle. I carried out a few turns with great caution and generally flew around for a while. I clearly remember looking at myself and at the wings more than once to make sure that it was not a dream! After about 15 to 20 minutes of flying, I turned towards the base, now hoping and praying that the landing would go well. As I approached the airfield, the neat concrete strip looked every bit the haven it is to pilots. (In later years, coming in to land with some emergency or in poor visibility, it was nothing less than exhilarating to see that strip of concrete straight ahead, like a mother opening her arms to her frightened child). I throttled back and descended to circuit height joining downwind for landing. I lined up on the final approach to the runway, dropping to get the correct glide angle.

As the aircraft came over the runway, I throttled back gradually and eased the stick back. Now, we were just off the ground and I continued to bring the stick slowly back to get a 3-point attitude for touchdown. But just as I was in this process, the main wheels touched the runway and the aircraft bounced. I held the stick steady, as taught by my instructor. Two further small bounces and we were firmly on the ground. The tail came down soon after, and I held the stick firmly back using the rudder to keep straight. The aircraft slowed down and I taxied back to the parking area and switched off. I felt as though the eyes of the whole world were upon me, celebrating my feat. My instructor was there to congratulate me. "Good show, my boy," he said, and put his arm around my shoulders. I said I was sorry for the bumpy landing, but he waved his hand in the air and said that it was pretty good for a first solo.

Through the coming months, we went through the various exercises that were intended to turn us wide-eyed flying enthusiasts into proper pilots. We did stalling, spinning, aerobatics, navigation and many other exercises to hone our pilot skills. Then came the final flying test with the Chief Flying Instructor. My CFI was one Squadron Leader Phillips. He was a soft-spoken and gentle officer, almost shy. I was thankful that he was taking my test, and not the other belligerent CFI.

During the briefing prior to the flight, he said he wanted me to carry out a normal flight, doing all I had learnt, and not to worry about his presence in the front cockpit, and indeed this did make me feel more at ease. We started up and went off into the sparkling blue sky and I carried out stalling, spinning, steep turns, loop, roll, roll off the top, and stall turns to either side. He then took the controls, closed throttle fully, and asked me to carry out a practice forced landing. As I overshot the chosen field, he said, "let us go home." We came back to the airfield, and I made a reasonably good landing. There was hardly a word from the CFI, and I was getting worried as to what he thought of my flying. We switched off and walked over to his office. He ordered two cups of tea, and waited till it was served and the orderly had left. By now I was really jittery, but the suspense did not last too long. He put his elbows on the table, cupped his chin and stared into my face for a few inordinately long seconds, and then uttered the most encouraging words: "Your flying was very nice." I was almost shocked to hear that, and I am sure it was his gentle and kind personality speaking. Nevertheless, it established a scale against which I could hereafter evaluate my performance. But his words, at such a critical stage in my flying career, meant more than he could possibly have imagined.

So ended my flying on the Tiger moth, an introduction to a delightful world of machines which are almost human, and which can throw challenges which are often superhuman. The Academy was to close for a few weeks of recess, during which period we could all go home, relax and get recharged for the next phase of flying on the more advanced aircraft - the Harvard 2B.

Harvard 2B

The Harvard was an all-metal aircraft, bigger, faster and more powerful. It had the looks of a World War II fighter: a large radial engine, a retractable under-carriage and a big variable pitch propeller. Even the sound of the engine was like a royal roar!

Once again, the old game of going solo on this advanced machine over-shadowed all other thoughts. In every course, there would normally be some suspensions at this stage also, though not as many as in the basic stage. Nevertheless, just the possibility of it was like a Damocles' sword hanging over our heads. Once you got through this solo stage, you were more or less cruising towards getting your wings – that hand-sewn white badge over the left breast pocket – a sign that you were special! And along with the wings, you would get the shoulder tapes of a Pilot Officer in the Indian Air Force, making you join the glorious family of young men, the likes of which you would not easily find elsewhere. And of course, you would get a salary of Rs. 475 per month, including Rs.150 as flying bounty (later called flying pay). The prospect was elevating, and the motivation immense.

The Harvard was a great teacher and not too forgiving either. It had a cunning capability of making you go round in circles – literally, that is, and that too on the ground! It had a tail wheel which was not lockable. This permitted the tail to swish sideways with the greatest of ease, thus throwing the aeroplane into a rapid and unwanted turn while on the landing run. If this motion was not controlled quickly by using the opposite rudder and brake, you would end up doing a 'ground loop', like a circle on the ground. If this happened at some reasonable speed, the aircraft could tilt sideways sufficiently for the outer wing tip to scrape the ground.

This was not only embarrassing in the extreme, but was considered outright ignominious. Anyone who permitted this to happen would be found walking back to the crew room with his head hanging down in shame. Also, if this happened more than say twice, you would probably be up for suspension. Thus, we did all we could to avoid such a predicament and I was lucky not to have one to my credit, or I should say debit.

After some ten flights of dual instruction, I found that the next day's flying programme, which was put up on the notice board in the mess, had the magic word 'solo' against my name. A shiver of excitement ran through me, and I stood gazing at the board for a while. Till I realised that others were waiting for me to move over.

Flying the Harvard solo after the Tiger Moth was like going from a tame pony to an elegant race horse. I remember that things definitely appeared to happen very fast on the Harvard. One had to rush through the cockpit checks on the downwind leg, otherwise you would overshoot the point where the turn onto the base leg was to commence, messing up the final approach for landing. However, it was not long before I was comfortable with the speed and relative complexity of the machine. In later years I would carry out tight curved approaches on numerous supersonic fighter aircraft, considerably faster and with relative ease, proving the point that the human mind has virtually unlimited potential and tremendous adaptability.

The cockpit of the Harvard was very spacious and the pupil flew from the front cockpit, the instructor being in the rear cockpit. Unlike the Tiger Moth, it had proper wheel brakes so there was no problem stopping the aircraft anytime. It also had landing flaps and trim tabs on the rudder and elevator. On the engine side, it had a propeller pitch control lever, in addition to the throttle and the mixture lever. It had a sliding hood, which was closed after take-off, so one could not feel the wind in the face for the most part of the flight.

In addition to the exercises we had done on the Tiger Moth, we carried out instrument flying, formation flying and night flying, all of which required much more practice, and a greater level of concentration. Night flying was quite an experience, as we did not have the type of runway lighting we have nowadays. We had only kerosene lamps called 'goose necks', which were placed along the edges of the runway at regular intervals. These were metal cans with long spouts, resembling the neck of a goose! The level of illumination provided by the flame was really meant only to indicate to the pilot where the edge of the runway lay, and not quite to enable him to actually see the surface on which he was to land. The instructors told us that while landing, if we felt the aircraft sinking for just a little bit longer than expected without making contact with the ground, we must open full throttle and go round, and make another attempt at landing.

For the first few solo landings, we were inclined to say a quick prayer after flaring out and closing throttle fully, desperately hoping to feel the concrete with the wheels. Soon enough we managed to make reasonably good three-point landings, also avoiding that devil of a swing. Now, with almost half a century of active flying to my credit, I would still hesitate to try a three-point landing at night on the Harvard with the bare minimum runway lighting we had then.

Formation flying was another unique experience, particularly when you do it for the first time. You have to use the stick and the throttle continuously to stay in the designated position, some 30 feet from the leader's aircraft. It requires a lot of practice to be able to do it well, but is a great thrill when you get it right. Initially, even to get a close air-to-air view of the other aircraft is pretty exciting. Some of our instructors would show-off by flying so close to the other aircraft that our wing tips touched gently.

The other important exercise which we were to carry out for the first time was instrument flying. For this purpose, we had to fly from the rear cockpit, with a hood over our heads, so that we could not see outside. Of course, the instructor would be in the front cockpit as a safety pilot. The hood, when drawn, simulated the condition of being in a cloud or flying in a dark night, where no outside cues would be available, and one would have to fly by reference to instrument readings alone.

To the layman, this may appear to be just another aspect of flying to be learnt through practice, but there is more to it than that. When you take away the visual cues from the pilot, his sense of balance or orientation is determined entirely by a very delicate balancing mechanism within the ears. This mechanism is easily fooled by the numerous random forces that the pilot's body is subjected to in the air. As a result, the feeling that the pilot gets about the aircraft's attitude can be different from what the instruments indicate. The instruments, of course, are telling the truth. But the pilot's feeling can be so overwhelming, that he is often disinclined to completely trust the instruments, leading to serious consequences. It's a battle royale, between a spontaneous animal response and cold human deliberation, where the pilot must choose the latter to win. During training as well as in subsequent practice, this aspect is drilled into the pilot's head, and indeed practice does help. But here, it is not a matter of just practice or skill or knowledge, or for that matter even experience. It is a matter of mental strength and self-discipline. There are many cases of pilot disorientation which have resulted in crashes, because the pilot has not been able to subdue his natural impulses. There are other aspects of flying, particularly fighter flying, where such mental fights have to be faced and won, for sheer survival.

On completion of our flying exercises, we were virtually assured of getting our wings, and there was a tangible sense of relief in the air. The final flying test was over and I had done well in it. There was a hush-hush talk of who would be put up for the flying trophy. Four of the best pilots would be chosen for the competition and would fly with different instructors, aiming to select the winner. My name did figure in the list, but finally the trophy went to someone else.

We had the graduation or 'passing out' parade as it was called, on 16th January 1954. The pinning of the coveted wings over the left breast pocket, and insertion of the Pilot Officer's tapes on the shoulder epaulettes was like a dream come true.

Our Commander-in-Chief was a British Air Marshal Gibbs. He was the one to take the salute and give us the wings and rank badges. As we came out of the parade, the first person to salute us was our Sergeant Major - the very person who till an hour or two ago, was the bully on the parade ground, and whose commands we had to execute without question. But now we were commissioned officers, and he was our subordinate. The reversal of roles was abrupt, and the sense of pride on his beaming face was touching testimony to the spirit of the armed forces, of the sense of duty and discipline, and the grace with which you place the interest of the service above your own. During my service career, I have seen this spirit of selfless devotion to duty so often; men work round the clock to achieve a given task, seeking nothing more than a simple pat on the back, if that. It is the foundation on which heroic struggles are made against formidable odds, and the reason why the Indian armed forces are considered to be among the finest in the world.

Just prior to the passing out parade, all cadets were asked to indicate which stream they would like to choose - fighters or transports, (there were no helicopters in the IAF or even in the country at that time). I opted for fighters, and as luck would have it, my most ardent wish was granted, and I was designated to the fighter stream. It is not that flying a transport plane is not enjoyable; indeed, it has its own charm, as I have subsequently found out. But there is no thrill that equals flying a good jet fighter: the speed and the power with which one can roam the skies, and the multitude of things you can do with the machine, is simply unmatched.

During the period of my flying training at IAF Academy in Begumpet, I formed a close friendship with my coursemate – Qaisar Ali. He was a very cultured and sensitive person, with old-world politeness and refined etiquette. We spent a lot of time together after the day's flying was done, and on weekends, we would ride our bicycles to town and have some *masala dosa* and *basundi*, and end up watching a movie.

After graduating as Pilot Officers, we went to IAF station Hakimpet to train on the sole jet fighter of the IAF at that time – the De Havilland Vampire. Here also, we shared a room in the Mess. At Hakimpet, a few horses were provided for the officers to go riding in the evenings. As we had both done riding in NDA, we took it up again eagerly, galloping our horses in the open grasslands on the shoulders of the runway and having a gala time!

After our short training on Vampire, we were both posted to different squadrons in Palam. From there, in due course, Qaisar went on to join a Canberra Squadron and later left the IAF to fly the big jets with Air India. Qaisar's friendship was a very special event in my life, and our relationship was based on deep understanding and mutual respect.

The First Jet Fighter of the IAF

Vampire 52

In August 1954, I was posted to No.1 Vampire Squadron at Palam, Delhi. The fighter aircraft opens up an enchanting world to a young pilot, and the sheer romance of it is overpowering. Having just 40 odd hours on the Vampire 52 fighter aircraft, I now looked forward to making a mark as a fighter pilot. It was a formidable challenge, one that called for focussing all my faculties to one single point, and then pushing it as far as it would go.

Those days, a Squadron Leader was the Squadron Commander, and would be in his early thirties. Flight Commanders were Flight Lieutenants, who would not easily speak to junior Pilot Officers like us. But the real tigers were the senior Flying Officers who ran the flying programme. They had 'arrived' and would rub that in as much as possible! As a junior pilot, my responsibility on ground was to update boards and charts in the flight office before pack-up. I made sure I completed the task even if it meant staying back after pack up time. My flying instructor had given me a gem of an advice: to keep my mouth shut and to take all tasks allotted to me seriously. This advice I followed almost to a fault, and the attitude of my seniors towards me soon changed to something like benevolence.

Our Squadron commander was Sqn Ldr "Timki" Brar, a regal figure, and our Flt Cdrs were Flt Lts SR Bose and AL Bajaj. There were around a dozen junior pilots including me.

The first few weeks in the squadron were devoted to honing our skills in formation flying. We had had some introductory training in this all important aspect of Fighter flying at Hakimpet, but now we had to prepare for air combat training. I remember my second sortie after joining the squadron: we did a two-aircraft formation take-off, and after some formation flying in different positions, did a wild and prolonged tail chase. TK 'Tikku' Sen was my leader, and by the time we came back, it was clear that he was mighty delighted with my performance. He was probably just two years older than me, if that, but very much the senior Flying Officer who ran the flying programme. He would often arrange to fly with me. He was an understanding and appreciative person, and made a big difference to my morale.

That was a time when the thought of being a fighter pilot – one of that special class – was so obsessive a thing that I was acutely conscious of it all the time. On many an occasion, a particularly good sortie would make me so overjoyed that I could not even sleep properly at night, thinking of the fascinating world waiting to be explored again the next day; it was a sweet disturbance!

Those early years in the squadron, most of us pilots in our early twenties, was a glorious time. There was this great romance with the aircraft and pride in being a part of an elite group, where courage and dash were the basic tools for success, and where one had to prove oneself every single day. Any young man's mind would be fired by such a challenge. Jet fighters were just arriving on the scene in India, and technology was at a manageable level, and did not dominate flying over much. Life was relatively simple and there was time and inclination for human relationships, and a tremendous desire for team work. The happiest memories I have of those days relate to doing things together – starting from flying, going out, or just sitting in the mess lawn in the evening and having a drink together. There was warmth and joy in the sense of togetherness, and faith in our collective future.

The Vampire 52 was the first jet fighter that the IAF acquired sometime around 1950. It was a British aircraft built by De Havilland Aircraft Company. It was somewhat unusual looking, with two booms extending to the rear and ending up in two small fins and rudders. Between the fins was one large tail plane which carried the elevator. It had a stubby fuselage made largely of wood, and a manually operated canopy. The aircraft had very little of a nose ahead of the pilot, thus giving a fantastic forward view, something that, later, only a MiG 23 or 27 could match. I still remember the light blue tint of the bullet-proof front windshield, which gave it an elitist look. It had manual flight controls and the good old elevator trim wheel on the left of pilot's seat. Undercarriage flaps and airbrakes were hydraulically operated, and the wheel brakes were pneumatic, that is working on air pressure, with the brake lever at the stick. The stick itself had a spade type grip, something I have not come across on any other fighter.

There were no navigation aids as such, other than a single radio set, which, had just four channels, at least on the initial versions. One had to take map- reading seriously if one were to avoid getting lost. There was no ejection seat, and the pilot had to carry his seat parachute to the aircraft every time he flew. The engine had no acceleration control and the pilot had to be careful in opening throttle to avoid engine surge. The aircraft was pressurized and could cruise merrily at 30,000 ft at a true airspeed of 300 knots, which was pretty fast those days. Another peculiar feature of the aircraft, at least in the earlier batches, was that it had five fuel gauges, one for each of its small tanks. So, whenever you wanted to check how much total fuel was left, you had to add up all the five readings, each being at a different level. I think it sharpened my mental arithmetic!

Another peculiarity of the aircraft was the loud rumble at the time of starting the engine, to minimize which the fuel cock had to be fiddled with skilfully. It was a great feeling if you managed to start without a rumble, but that was not often. It could carry two 1,000 pound bombs under its wings or two rocket launchers. It also had four guns of 20 mm calibre embedded in the front fuselage. A gyro gunsight of World War II vintage enabled aiming of the weapons. It could, if required, also carry two 100 gallon drop tanks.

I learnt much of my fighter flying on the Vampire; we did a lot of air-to-ground gunnery, rocketry and bombing since Tilpat firing range was close by. We also did a lot of air-to-air cine work, where you carry out mock attacks on another aircraft and film it. There were films taken during the air to ground attacks as well. Every morning, before the commencement of flying, the previous day's films would be screened and critical comments made by the Flight Commander, and some pilot would get a dressing down for errors made. All these comments would be entered in the Blue Book of the pilot, going on record. We were assessed for every single flight and naturally, there was a tremendous eagerness to do well. This kept us on our toes all the time and ensured a high level of motivation, so important at the learning stage.

There was always a special atmosphere in the Squadron whenever 'range' work was in progress. The ground crew would be busy turning the aircraft around, and loading up the guns, rockets or bombs. An array of trolleys and other ground equipment would be lying scattered over the tarmac. Our Flight Commander, Flt. Lt. Chhota Bose, who was also one of the early Pilot Attack Instructors, would strut about giving instructions to the ground crew to get the aircraft ready for the next detail. He would often walk up to a pilot already strapped up in the cockpit, and give him the latest 'gunsight' picture to hold at the time of firing. For Bose *Sahib*, as he was referred to by us junior pilots, flying and all that goes with it, was religion. He was a hard task master and a thorough professional. As often happens with people who are deeply committed, he could not tolerate slackness in anyone and would easily lose his temper. But he was so sincere and almost childlike in his demeanour, that it was impossible to hold it against him. We loved and respected him greatly, and even came to enjoy his thick Bengali accent. Much of what I learnt about fighter flying in those early days I owe to him.

The Vampire was a subsonic aircraft, meaning its maximum speed was less than the speed of sound, that is below about 760 mph. However, it was possible to dive it to 0.8 Mach, which is 80 per cent of the speed of sound. But when one reached this speed, some parts of the wing would encounter airflow which was close to Mach 1. This caused 'shock waves' to be generated, which caused a kind of turmoil in the airflow over the wings, which played havoc with the stability and controllability of the aircraft. The aircraft would buck up and down like a naughty horse, and the feel of the controls would become weird, making it extremely difficult to keep it on a straight path. As young fighter pilots, we had to put the aircraft into that condition deliberately, and learn to recover safely.

Initially, it was a somewhat uncomfortable experience, and one had to push oneself to do it. But it helped in developing the much needed confidence, a commodity no fighter pilot can do without. I made a firm commitment to push myself to do precisely the manoeuvres I felt most reluctant to carry out. It was a kind of private resolve, and it was not always comfortable to carry it out. Yet, it was the only way to keep a step ahead of the aircraft.

In the mid-fifties, Palam airfield was a relatively peaceful place controlled by the Air force. Four squadrons were located here: Number 1 Vampire Squadron, to which I belonged, Number 10 Vampire Night Fighter Squadron, a Photo Reconnaissance Squadron having Spitfire Mark 19 aircraft, and the Communication Squadron with transport aircraft for carrying VIPs.

Much of the flying at the airfield was of military aircraft, with only an occasional Indian Airlines flight. I still remember the early morning take off of the Indian Airlines Viking aircraft. This was a two engine propeller aircraft, and the pilots, probably ex-IAF, would invariably do a low undercarriage retraction, which looked very thrilling to us. At that time, the only jet aircraft in the country was the Vampire fighter flown by us, something that definitely enhanced our sense of self importance!

Once, I was detailed to ferry a Vampire fighter aircraft from Begumpet to Kanpur. It was monsoon time, so the route was expected to be fairly cloudy. However, the meteorological report had not predicted any cumulonimbus clouds en-route. These are the massive towering clouds which are behind all thunderstorms, and are monsters of immense turbulence, lightning and hail, as well as icing. Pilots are strongly advised not to enter them. The weather radars of modern aircraft are meant primarily to detect these monsters.

The Vampire aircraft, however, was a single-seat jet fighter of early vintage, and had neither weather radar, nor indeed any navigation system. The only help was a radio to enable contact with the ground, when within range. In other words, when you are up there and away from base, you were well and truly on your own, and God help you! Navigation had to be carried out with the help of a hand held map, a clock and a good dose of mental arithmetic! Of course, if inside clouds, you cannot see anything outside, and hence a map is no use till you break cloud and the ground is visible.

I took off from Begumpet for the two- hour flight to Kanpur in the morning and climbed to the cruising altitude of 30,000 ft. There were some layers of broken clouds here and there, but the space ahead looked reasonably clear. About 45 minutes into the flight, I got into some thin, smooth clouds which seemed innocuous enough. I had to get onto flying on instruments, which at this stage, was no real problem. However, gradually and almost imperceptibly, the clouds started getting darker, and somewhat more turbulent. This carried on for a while till I was past the halfway mark. That is when the turbulence increased and I wondered if I might be unwittingly entering one of those dreaded cumulonimbus clouds, possibly hidden behind the soft facade. I was still hopeful that it may be a small one and manageable, since the Met report had not issued any such warning. My hopes were, however, well and truly dashed when a blinding flash of lightning welcomed my arrival, followed by a hearty dose of thunder, lashing rain and whipping air currents which rocked the airplane and sent my pulse racing. I was already past the halfway mark, so it was too late to turn back. I had no choice but to stick in there, grit my teeth and hope for the best.

Soon, it became so dark in the cockpit that I had to turn on all cockpit lights. It was a great struggle to keep the aircraft flying straight and level, and only on instruments. As if that was not enough, I felt hail hitting the canopy with a heavy patter, off and on. I prayed that it does not shatter the canopy and plunge me into the low pressure and a temperature of minus 20 degrees C outside. In addition, there was the possibility of disorientation. I did experience this phenomenon to some degree but strict deliberation kept it under check.

It was a veritable ride through hell for a good 30 minutes, during which time the aircraft would have covered some 150 miles. A fully developed cumulonimbus cloud cluster could well be up to 250 miles wide, extending from a height of 500 ft to over 50,000 ft. It is a real monster, and behaves like one. Ice can also form on the wings, and drastically degrade its aerodynamics. If a lot of it gets sucked into the air intake, engine failure was also a real possibility. In other words, everything at that moment is against you!

After such a long time in cloud with no idea of my ground position, I was also worried how I would locate Kanpur airfield before my fuel ran out. The heavens must have heard my plea of distress for I suddenly broke cloud into bright sunlight and a beautiful blue sky. I looked back and saw this mountain of a cloud towering over us like a gigantic wall. I had to quickly fix my ground position, not an easy task after such a long time in cloud. As I banked the aircraft left and right to look for a recognizable ground feature, I noticed a beautiful elbow of a bend in a stream running along our flight path, which I knew was near a town called Banda. Hurrah! I had made it. This town was some 100 miles from our position and I knew how to reach Kanpur from there. Soon I was able to get into radio contact with Kanpur air traffic control, and commenced my descent for a safe landing. Thank the Lord!

Weapons Training

In November 1954, the whole squadron moved to Jamnagar for comprehensive weapons training. A special train was arranged to carry all the ground equipment as well as the ground crew, while all 16 aircraft of the squadron were flown to Jamnagar in formations of four aircraft each. IAF station, Jamnagar, was not well established in terms of accommodation, and we had to operate from tents pitched near the tarmac. The Officer's Mess was of brick construction but our living quarters were tents, manned by our personal batman.

The armament training was spread over some three months, during which time each pilot was to do about 50 hours of flying. The very first phase was air-to-air cine work and was devoted to carrying out different types of attacks on another aircraft in the air, and filming it for evaluation of aiming accuracy. This was followed by live gun firing on a target drogue towed by a Dakota transport aircraft. This was quite a unique and exciting exercise. The drogue was about 20 feet long with a diameter of three feet or so. It was made of white canvas and had black stripes on it to make it more prominent. The Dakota, which towed it, was painted a bright yellow for easy detection, and the drogue would trail 250 feet or so behind it on a cable. Our firing zone was over a particular stretch of the sea close to the coast, where no shipping or other activity was permitted. The Dakota would fly parallel to the coast, some two miles into the sea, and we had to fire on the drogue pointing towards the sea. The air was generally very smooth over the water and we had to make sure that we fired at some reasonable angle to the drogue to avoid pointing our guns towards the Dakota. Whenever the bullets hit the drogue, it would shudder in a characteristic manner and the pilot would know that he had scored some hits. It was always a great feeling when you caused the shudder. I was the top scorer in the squadron with 26 per cent bullet hits, which is supposed to be pretty good for air- to- air firing on this small target.

The next phase was air-to-ground gun firing, rocket firing and bombing. The air-to-ground range was located on a marshy bit of desolate land close to the coast near the airfield. All firing was done pointing towards the sea. The target for gun firing was 10 feet by 10 feet of white canvas mounted on a metal frame and tilted 60 degrees to face the attacking aircraft in the dive. There would normally be four such targets lined up side by side with some 150 feet spacing. A pilot would be allotted one of these numbered targets, and would be allowed six to eight attacks in a sortie. When the guns are fired, the pilot might see the bullets hitting the ground close to the target but missing it. He would then make necessary corrections to his aim when he came in for the next attack. When the bullets hit the target properly, one would only see some dust rising from behind the target and not the impact points. It was thrilling to have a good burst, and see only some dust rising from behind the target. Once you were done with firing, the Range Safety Officer would drive over in his jeep to the target and count all fresh bullet holes and paint them black. The target would then be ready for the next pilot's attacks. A simple and easy method to count the score of each pilot. By the time you landed back and reached the flight office, your score would already have been passed on telephone. It was an exciting and suspenseful moment, and one would feel great if the score was good. I averaged a good score, and the highest in the squadron at 47 per cent for a total of some 700 bullets fired.

For rocket firing and bombing, the target was a white circle of 20 yards radius, etched on the ground. It had a well marked centre point, called the 'pin', which is what one aimed at. If you hit the pin, it was called a 'direct hit'. This would not happen often, but when it did, your day was made. The point of impact of the rocket or bomb was determined geometrically by directional readings from three different observation posts, called quadrants, located around the target at a safe distance. The meeting point of the three directional readings would determine the impact point of the rocket or bomb. If the lines did not meet at a single point, they would make a small triangle; in which case the centre point of the triangle would be taken to be the impact point. Before the pilot came round for the next attack, he would be told over the radio, the bearing and distance of the last impact point from the pin in clock code, e.g.: "3 o'clock 10 yards", which would mean the rocket or bomb hit the ground 10 yards to the right of the pin. In aviation parlance, frequent use is made of this clock code to indicate direction. Thus, 12 o'clock would be straight ahead in front, and 6 o'clock directly behind and so on. It is a useful method.

My average error for rocket firing was 12 yards, and for bombing it was between 10 and 30 yards depending on the type of bombing. These were considered to be reasonably good scores. And so ended happily my first test of weapon delivery on fighter aircraft.

To Halwara

We finished our armament training at Jamnagar by end January 1955 and flew via Jodhpur to Halwara, near Ludhiana in Punjab, where we were to operate from for a year. As we commenced our descent, we could spot the airstrip from some 20 miles - a clean concrete strip right in the midst of miles and miles of green mustard fields, topped with bright yellow flowers. It was a beautiful sight, especially after the dry countryside around Jamnagar.

At that time, Halwara was a non-family station, and only one squadron could be positioned there at any given time. There was no pucca living accommodation for us officers, and we had to live in tents located on the banks of a nearby canal full of water. My tent-mate was one of my course mates, SP Singh, a good friend of mine.

Our tent was small and pretty cramped. Two cots were placed parallel along the two sides, and the only other furniture that could fit in was a bedside table next to each cot. Our toilets were a line of trenches dug deep in the ground at some distance, and partitioned by vertical canvas panels, like camping. It was a primitive way of living, but we took to it with excitement, especially since there was not much to do here other than the flying.

SP Singh was from rural Punjab, and his father was a farmer who lived in a nearby village called Banur, somewhere between Ludhiana and Ambala. SP, as we called him, had run away from home at a young age, surviving on odd jobs and somehow managing to educate himself and got selected for the IAF as a pilot. A really self-made man, SP also owned a 3.5 hp motorcycle and was my advisor on buying a second hand bike. He spotted one 3.5 hp maroon BSA for sale and I dished out Rs 2,000 or so for it, wiping out my meagre bank balance! On weekends, we would often bike down to Ludhiana town, some 20 miles away, along with other friends, and enjoy a sumptuous meal at a dhaba. Simple joys!

At Halwara, the squadron concentrated on tactical and combat exercises. We did a lot of low-level tactical formations, where four aircraft would get airborne and fly in battle formation and navigate towards a chosen target, often a road or railway bridge in the countryside. On reaching the target, we would pull up one behind the other and carry out mock bomb or rocket attacks diving on to the target, re-group back into formation and return to base. While flying low over the countryside, we would at times chance upon vast expanses of ripening wheat fields shimmering in the sun--a bountiful golden vista- that would fill our hearts with joy and pride.

In Halwara, we also carried out a lot of mock air combat exercises called 'one-versus-one'. Here, two aircraft would get airborne in formation and climb up to a height of 15,000 feet or so. They would then split and get a kilometre or so apart, abreast of each other. The leader would then countdown to commence the fight, calling on the radio: "three, two, one, now". Both aircraft would then turn towards each other and try to get behind the adversary. In a fight against an enemy aircraft, it is crucial to get behind him before he can – this ensures that your missiles or guns are pointing at him, while his are pointing away from you - a safe position to make a kill. Vigorous manoeuvring is done to secure such a coveted position. The aircraft in front would, of course, do its best to shake off the enemy from the tail, thus leading to a 'tail chase'. Since this is what contending dogs do, such a fight is called a 'dog fight'! It is presumed that the aircraft in front would be 'shot down' by the one behind. It is a stressful and vigorous exercise that teaches profound lessons in air combat, and is a regular item on the menu in fighter squadrons.

xxxxxx

On some silent and still afternoons, I would take a stroll by myself to a nearby grove of profusely flowering Amaltas trees. The golden glow and tender aroma of the flowers, among the twittering of little birds in the merriment of spring, would evoke in me a profound sense of beauty and peace. Those were precious moments.

xxxxxx

Our squadron stayed for a relatively short time at Halwara before being ordered back to Palam, our home base. I remained in the squadron for a year more before being detailed for a Flying Instructors course at Tambaram near Chennai. This was a six month course, which would make you a Qualified Flying Instructor (QFI). Thereafter, you would be posted to one of the flying academies, either at Begumpet, Secunderabad or Jodhpur. Your job there would be to teach young flight cadets, who aspire to become IAF pilots, how to fly.

This also meant that you would be off fighters for some years, flying only light piston-engine machines. I was quite disappointed in being pulled out of my squadron, but had to follow orders. We had two types of aircraft on the Flying Instructor's course: an HT-2 (Hindustan Trainer), which was designed and manufactured by HAL, Bangalore, and the faster Harvard. We were each given a book on instructional technique, which contained in great detail, how to talk to the cadet while giving him instructions in the air. The actual words and phrases to be used were clearly indicated. We were expected to learn these by heart and use them during our 'patter' (i.e. talk in the air). Two of us would get airborne together in one machine – one would act as an instructor and the other as a cadet. And we would practice this patter while giving instructions on the various phases of the flight. This carried on for two months or so, and I was getting royally bored when Providence again came to my rescue.

One evening at weekend party in the mess, the duty officer of the day came up to me and said there was an urgent message for me from Air Headquarters. He gave me the 'signal' which I opened with some trepidation. It said: "You have been selected to proceed to France for conversion on the Mystere IV aircraft. Report to Air HQ as early as possible." I was overjoyed to be pulled out half way through the course to get back to fighter flying, and that too on the latest transonic fighter aircraft of the time. And to France! It was like being suddenly transported from a boring class room into a sparkling blue sky, from purring piston engine machines to thundering fighter jets! What a great lift!

The First Transonic Jet Fighter of the IAF

Mystere

There were ten pilots selected for Mystere conversion: Sqn Ldr Dilbagh Singh, Flt Lts Omi Taneja, Bhattacharya, Basu and RV Singh, and Flg Offrs Chini Mehta, P Ashoka, Mangat, Omi Mathur and Sridharan. We all had to leave for France in October 1956. It was already early September and we had to rush to Ambala for quick familiarization flights on the Toofani (Dassault Ouragan fighter), before leaving.

Those days, Air India did not have any jet aircraft, and we travelled to France by a Super Constellation – a four piston engine powered airliner of great beauty and prestige. We spent a day in Paris completing some formalities with the Air Attaché and then proceeded to Dijon, *Armée de l'Air Française* (French Air force) base for Mystere squadrons.

Dijon was a relatively small town those days, close to the German and Swiss borders, and famous for its mustard. The month of October was spent primarily in preparation for flying the Mystere - with detailed lectures and briefings on the various systems of the aircraft, its flying characteristics, and emergency procedures.

The Mystere was one of the first operational transonic aircraft in the world, along with the British Hunter and the American Sabre jet. It could go beyond the speed of sound (Mach 1.0) in a dive. In order to achieve this, it had a few special design features. The most obvious was the shape of its wings, which were relatively thin and swept back at an angle of around 40 degrees to make it look like an arrowhead. This reduced the aerodynamic drag at high speeds and enabled it to cross the sound barrier more easily. The other significant feature was that it had fully 'powered' flight controls, a novel feature at that time. This meant that when the pilot moved his control stick (or rudder pedals), he did not directly move the control surface, but merely operated a valve, which sent hydraulic fluid under high pressure into the hydraulic jacks of the control surface, which in turn moved the control surface in the appropriate direction.

In normal manually controlled aircraft like the Vampire, the pilot has to manually move the control surface against air resistance – the higher the speed, the greater the air resistance, and hence, higher the force he has to apply. Thus, on high-speed aircraft, if powered controls were not provided, the pilot would encounter very high stick forces, which would not only tire him, but also undermine manoeuvrability of the aircraft. Therefore, all high-speed aircraft, and particularly fighters, must have powered flight controls. Of course, this also makes the controls very sensitive. In addition, the aerodynamics of high-speed aircraft are quite different from those of slower aircraft. Thus, flying transonic power controlled aircraft required somewhat special flying techniques. And, since Mystere did not have a two-seat trainer, we just had to leap into the air and learn for ourselves! It was somewhat daunting, but exciting all the same.

In early November 1956, with great excitement, I got airborne on my first solo on the Mystere. I found the flight controls to be delightfully light; the aircraft responding superbly. I carried out a few rapid rolls with just a flick of my wrist--what a pleasure. It was love at first feel! I completed the flight as briefed and managed a reasonably good landing.

Each one of our pilots flew 20 to 25 flights to get familiar with the machine. We also flew in formation and did some tail chases and dog fights. I remember one flight in a four- aircraft formation, where the other three pilots were from the French Air force. Our leader led us on a low level tactical sortie and we crossed over into Germany and mock-attacked one of their airfields. I was not even briefed about it, and merely followed the leader, with some apprehension!. Many of the French pilots were Sergeant Pilots, good flyers, but not entirely well disciplined.

xxxxxx

We used to commute to work in a Tram in the company of many modest folks going for work. I remember how we would always offer our seats to some old folks or a lady with a small baby, and receive a grateful smile from the person, amid approving nods from other passengers. A heart warming experience to start the day with!

xxxxxx

There were a few things that made us feel that we were really flying a high-speed aircraft. One was the relatively higher climbing speed – 420 knots at lower altitudes and 0.85 Mach at higher altitudes. The term 'Mach' itself was a source of excitement and pride, since it was indicative of being close to the speed of sound. On the Mystere, we could climb to 40,000 ft on a regular basis, which was way above the 30,000 feet limit on Vampires and Toofanis. What is more, during climb beyond 35,000ft, we would reach 'trail height', where a white condensation trail would appear behind each aircraft. This was the result of the low outside temperature along with low pressure, which would cause the moisture in the hot exhaust gasses of the engine to condense into water and ice particles, making a long white plume. It was a beautiful sight and a great novelty initially.

We returned from France in March 1957, and in April, Flt. Lt. Bhattacharya (Bhattu) and I were posted to Aircraft Erection Unit at Santa Cruz airport in Bombay. Our boss was Sqn. Ldr Bhupinder (Bindi) Singh, a veteran Test Pilot. Mystere aircraft from France were shipped to Bombay in a dismantled condition, and were to be reassembled at this unit. We would test fly the aircraft and keep them ready for being ferried to Kalaikunda near Kharagpur in West Bengal, where my old No.1 Squadron was to be formed with the new aircraft.

Since the Mystere was the first transonic aircraft to come to the country, we enjoyed creating sonic booms over Bombay, which would promptly be reported in the evening papers! As Santa Cruz airport had very little air traffic those days, the control tower would often ask us to show some low-level aerobatics over the airfield. This request was acceded to with pleasure. Our displays with the aircraft would invariably end with a high speed run at a low level over the runway.

On May 11, 1957, I came in for the high speed run at the end of the flight and was in a shallow dive approaching along the runway at about 550 knots, when suddenly I hit severe turbulence. The aircraft pitched up and down violently, and as a pilot's reflex, I tried to control it. In the process, I went 'out of phase', the pitching oscillations became aggravated, and I lost control. We had been briefed in France that the only way to recover from such oscillations was to leave the controls and let the aircraft's stability get you out of it. I eased back on the stick (to ensure that we did not descend and hit the ground), and then left the controls. The aircraft recovered on its own, and I realized that I had blacked out for a while due to the high 'g' forces, up and down. My crash helmet had come down over my face and I had to push it up to be able to see. I reduced speed and regained level flight. I noticed that I had deep bleeding cuts on both my shins just above the ankles. The severe oscillations had flayed my legs up and down, hitting them vigorously against the bottom edge of the instrument panel. I also had a pain in my neck, and could not hold my head straight – I guess it too must have bobbed up and down during the oscillations, thus spraining my neck. My shoulder straps had also caused severe chafing on my shoulders. I was definitely shaken but landed back safely.

What I had encountered was pilot-induced-oscillations (PIO for short), which is a known phenomenon on high-speed aircraft with powered flight controls. It occurs on account of over-sensitivity of the longitudinal control at high speeds and particularly at lower altitudes. There are aircraft systems available today which regulate the sensitivity of the controls with an increase in speed to prevent such oscillations. All modern high-speed fighter aircraft have such systems. However, in those early days of high-speed aircraft, such systems were still in the process of development and the Mystere did not have the full benefit of this technology. The pilot had to be extremely gentle with the controls at high speeds to avoid such oscillations. I had obviously not been careful enough. High-speed fighters are a delight to fly, but boy, can they bite!

Since, during the oscillations the aircraft had exceeded the structural 'g' limit by a big margin (it sustained 12g against the limit of 7g), it had to be sent to No.1 Base Repair Depot (BRD) at Kanpur for a thorough check-up and necessary repairs. When they dismantled the aircraft, they found that the main wing spars (i.e. the main load-bearing beams) had got bent, and had to be reinforced. For some reason, the repairs got delayed and were completed only some years later, by which time I was posted to BRD Kanpur as a Test Pilot, and I had the pleasure of flight testing that very aircraft (IA 940), and clearing it.

The term 'g' is used very often in fighter flying, and it is worthwhile understanding its manifestations. The letter 'g' stands for acceleration due to gravity, which is 32 feet per second, every second. It is this acceleration which gives us our weight. In an aircraft, the centrifugal force that is caused in a turn or in pitching results in a similar acceleration. And just as the acceleration due to gravity translates into weight, in a similar way the acceleration caused by the centrifugal force, can be expressed in terms of weight. Thus 2 'g' would mean twice the acceleration caused by gravity, and would result in twice the weight as experienced by the pilot. At any given speed, the tighter the aircraft turns, the higher is the centrifugal force, and so also the 'g' experienced by the pilot.

In air combat, the aircraft which can turn tighter has a clear advantage over its adversary, and can out-manoeuvre him and get into a position to shoot him down. Hence, modern fighter aircraft are built structurally strong enough to withstand up to 10 'g', enabling them to turn very tightly even at high speeds, with consequent advantage in combat. The fighter pilot is thus subjected to very high 'g' forces in combat. At 8 'g', which is the sort of 'g' a present day fighter pilot may encounter in combat, his weight temporarily becomes eight times his normal weight. Such manifold increase in weight causes immense stress on his bone structure and muscles and pins him down to his seat, virtually immobilizing him. At high 'g', it is not easy for the pilot to raise his arm or head. Hence, all the essential controls for firing his weapons need to be positioned close to his fingers on the throttle and stick, so that he can operate them during combat without moving his hand. This is called HOTAS, which stands for 'Hands on Throttle and Stick'. Such a provision is essential for success in air combat.

At high 'g's, the blood from the pilot's head flows down to lower parts of his body, resulting in temporary loss of vision, which of course, is unacceptable during air combat. In order to minimize this effect, fighter pilots have to wear special 'g' suits. These are tight-fitting suits which have expandable air channels and air bags built into them. A hose connects these channels to a valve on the aircraft, which opens progressively as the 'g' increases, supplying high pressure air to the channels, and expanding them. This results in the 'g' suit clinging more tightly to the pilot's torso and restricting the downward flow of blood from his head, minimizing vision loss. In some fighter aircraft, the pilot's seat is inclined backwards to minimize the flow of blood away from his head in high 'g' manoeuvres, enabling him to retain his vision at higher 'g' values.

In addition to this, at high 'g', the pilot's body gets forced into a crouching position, compressing his rib cage and restricting the space for the lungs to expand. He thus has to resort to short and shallow breaths like a panting dog, literally. One can see how tough a fighter pilot's job is!

xxxxxx

By June '57, all aircraft had been ferried to Kalaikunda to form the first Mystere No.1 Tiger Squadron, also the first transonic squadron of the Indian air force. I had the privilege of being one of the first few pilots to break the sound barrier over Indian soil.

Kalaikunda base itself was brand new, and our squadron was the first to be positioned there. It had a long concrete runway on one side, and all the hangars and buildings on the other side. Beautiful, gleaming taxi tracks connected the aircraft parking tarmac to the runway – a most inviting sight for us young pilots, only too eager to get airborne in our silver birds.

While the buildings for the squadron, as well as the administration offices, were complete and ready for occupation, there was no Mess building or proper living quarters for bachelor officers yet. We lived in a few vacant married officers' quarters until our quarters came up a year later.

As expected, all ten pilots who had returned from France were posted to the squadron. Sqn. Ldr. Dilbagh Singh was our C.O. and Flt. Lts. Omi Taneja and Bhattacharya were our Flight Commanders. Flying was great fun, not only because of our high performance machines, but also because all the pilots were chosen for their flying ability. As a result, everyone knew exactly what to do in the air. We did a lot of tactical formation flying and it was a pleasure to have perfect understanding between the members of the formation. There were occasions when even a detailed briefing was not done prior to takeoff. All that the leader said was to follow the SOP (Standard Operating Procedure). One day, I led a four aircraft formation on a low level tactical sortie. After completing the tactical part, I ordered the four aircraft to get into a tight 'box' formation, which looks like an arrow head. I did a few turns and wing overs, and then just dived and pulled her up into a loop without warning. We completed the loop in perfect formation, then came back and landed one behind the other. As we were walking back to the crew room, there were wide smiles on everyone's face for the trust I had placed on their flying ability. We had terrific team spirit which made flying together a joyous experience.

Other than the high speed aerodynamic shape and powered flight controls, the Mystere also had a few other sophistications common to high performance fighter aircraft. It was the first aircraft in the IAF to have a tail parachute, also called braking parachute. This was deployed after landing to decelerate the aircraft rapidly. It was a very effective device, and one felt a solid tug when it was deployed. On the Mystere, it also caused a significant nose-up pitching, so the pilot had to briskly push the stick forward to counter it. The parachute was operated by a single switch handily located on the throttle – one click deployed it, and when, after slowing down, the pilot wanted to jettison it, it merely required one more click on the same switch – typical French finesse!

The Mystere also had, for the first time in the IAF, an anti-skid device on the brakes. This permits the pilot to apply full brakes after landing, without the fear of locking the wheels and bursting the tyres. The system automatically releases the brakes just prior to reaching a pre-determined level of deceleration on the wheels which could cause locking. The brakes would come on again once the deceleration eased up a bit, and release again if full brakes were still on. Consequently, the aircraft would keep jerking in the process of slowing down. The cooling of the brakes was rather inadequate. Quite often they would smoke due to overheating, giving out a surprisingly pleasant smell of burnt brake material. Of course, if the tail parachute was deployed, there was no chance of brakes getting over-heated. We, however, tried to avoid using the tail chute as far as possible to minimize the work of the maintenance staff.

We also discovered that holding the aircraft in an exaggerated nose up attitude just after landing, created significant aerodynamic drag, and decelerated the aircraft rapidly, thus requiring much less braking effort and preventing the brakes from overheating. This type of aerodynamic braking is most noticeable on swept wing aircraft with low wings. The Mystere was quite a classic example in this regard, and the more experienced pilots routinely resorted to this technique.

Other than tactical flying, we had the usual gun firing practice at a range near Balasore, on the coast of the Bay of Bengal. There was a stretch of flat beach of dark clay, where the targets would be erected, and we would fire in a north-easterly direction along the beach. The white canvas targets would stand out against the dark clay, and it was a pretty sight when you first spotted it. Being a flat beach, we had to do our firing only during low tide. The clay would be wet and shining, and often the bullets would just dig in without kicking up any mud. We would thus not know if we had hit the target at all! Only after landing, when we got our scores, would the suspense abate!

Once I was detailed as the Range Safety Officer (RSO) for a session of firing over a few days. I went by road to Balasore, and was put up in a small army mess near the beach – a lonely but lovely outpost. At that time, I was the only officer in the mess, with one cook and one batman to look after my needs. There were numerous Casuarina trees around the mess building, constantly hissing in the sea breeze, giving a rather eerie feeling at night!

The cook would ask me what I wanted for the next meal and would faithfully rustle it up, and set the table complete with proper crockery and cutlery. It was a refreshing break for me from the hustle and bustle of squadron life. I would, of course, have preferred to be firing at the targets rather than counting the holes in it!

Another novelty on the Mystere was the provision of radar ranging. This small radar fitted in the nose of the aircraft gave the pilot the exact distance of the target aircraft to enable accurate firing. On earlier aircraft like Vampire and Toofani, the pilot had to visually judge the distance, a difficult task and prone to errors.

One of Mystere's strong points was the lethality of its armament. In addition to two 30 mm cannons built into the nose of the aircraft, it could carry two bombs or two pods of special 68 mm rockets, one under each wing. Each of these pods carried 19 rockets. These rockets were relatively small and sleek, and attained a high velocity before impact. When these pods were fired, all 19 rockets would blast off in one go, giving a terrific anti-tank capability. In addition to the two pods, another 55 such rockets were carried inside the fuselage on a rack just under the cockpit. When the pilot pressed the trigger, the whole rack would descend down and all 55 rockets would fire off in two seconds. Thus, the fire power of the Mystere was formidable, and played havoc against Pakistani tanks in the 1965 war, ensuring a few Vir Chakras for the squadron.

I remember one flight, where I was called up on the radio to return to base immediately as heavy rain was approaching. I promptly set course but I was some distance away. By the time I reached the airfield, an intense thunder-shower was lashing down on the base. It did not look as if the rain would abate in a hurry, and I did not have enough fuel to divert or to delay my landing too much. I thus had no choice but to attempt a landing in the rain. It was a tricky situation, as in a fighter aircraft, visibility from the cockpit is extremely poor under such conditions. I had great difficulty spotting the runway as there was no ground radar to help. It was my good luck that through the translucent wind-shield, I caught a glimpse of a mildly shining strip - the runway - and I managed to line-up for landing. Now, the problem was to judge my height visually to make a safe landing. It was pouring heavily and my outside view was badly blurred, so it was very difficult to judge my height accurately to touch down safely on the runway, but I somehow managed it and deployed the tail parachute. The aircraft skidded right and left due to the thick layer of water on the runway surface, causing what is called 'aqua-planing', but I did not go off the runway. My CO and flight commanders were all in the flying control watching me land in such conditions. It was a great relief to get back in one piece and not have had to eject.

Once, another squadron mate and I decided to make a round trip to Mount Everest in two Mysteres. We managed to get both our names down on the flying programme for a general flying sortie in the same time block. I brought my camera to take some shots. Mount Everest is located some 250 miles north of Kalaikunda on the northern border of Nepal. We got airborne as planned, joined up in the air and headed north. Sometime after we reached an altitude of 40,000 ft and settled down to a cruise, we could see the tip of a solitary peak shining in the morning sunlight. It had to be Mount Everest!

So we pointed our aircraft towards it. In 20 to 25 minutes we were over hilly terrain with patches of snow over some of the smaller peaks and in a matter of 10 minutes we were over the magnificent peak shining gloriously pink in the morning sky – an awe inspiring sight! We circled the peak once, and I took some shots with my camera. We had to set course immediately for base as we did not have enough fuel to stay there longer. As we headed back, I could see nothing but smaller snow-clad peaks all around. We had not noticed how deep we had gone into the Himalayan ranges, because of the haze. Now that the haze had abated, we could see more clearly, and it was a bit worrying to be so deep into such remote and inhospitable terrain in a single engine aircraft. We spent some lengthy minutes just keeping a watch on our engine parameters. However, our aircraft behaved perfectly and we landed back safely without anyone suspecting what tricks we had been up to.

Flypast

Our Mystere squadron took part in the Republic Day flypast in Delhi for the first time in January 1958. We ferried all 16 aircraft from Kalaikunda to Palam in formations of four. It was a grand sight to see all 16 gleaming, swept wing Mysteres parked in a neat line on the tarmac at Palam. This was also the first time high performance aircraft were on display at Delhi, and we made some headlines.

For the flypast, we were to fly in four 'box' formations of four aircraft each, one box behind the other, at a fixed distance. The radio call signs of the four boxes were: Mystere Red, Mystere Blue, Mystere Yellow and Mystere Green. Once all aircraft had started up, our leader, Sqn. Ldr. Dilbagh Singh, would call for a radio check, and all aircraft would respond in sequence: Red 2, Red 3, Red 4, Blue 1, Blue 2, and so on till the last pilot called Green 4. It was a great feeling to have all the aircraft responding in perfect sequence and with precise time gaps; it reinforced our team spirit. When we taxied out one behind the other, we would maintain an exact gap of 50 yards between aircraft. The take offs would be in pairs, joining up with the other pair to form the box. All four boxes would proceed to a rendezvous point and make a few orbits there, one box behind the other, and set course to fly over Rajpath at a precise time. It had to be real precision flying, as any error beyond a few seconds would upset the following formations, and would evoke unpleasant reactions.

Initially, a few practice flypasts were held over Palam, and all formations were filmed from the ground. During the debriefing, the photographs would be projected on a screen to see how good the formations looked. The Mystere formations came in for praise every time for their neatness, as well as for their well-disciplined performance all round. We all felt justly proud of our squadron and our speed birds.

In those years, the Republic Day flypast would comprise a total of 100 odd aircraft, and naturally, would involve over 100 pilots, all gathering at Palam, and making it a grand social occasion. The high speed Mystere pilots would receive special attention, with questions about the aircraft performance and other special features. There would, of course, be a 'riot' in the evenings at the bar, everyone greatly enjoying the get-together before we returned to our base in Kalaikunda.

I had disposed of my BSA bike before proceeding to France and was looking for another second hand bike in Kalaikunda. My friend Chini Mehta came to learn about someone in Kharagpur town wanting to sell his bike. We neither knew its make nor the price, but landed up at this gentleman's house to check. He welcomed us and took us to his side-verandah, where the bike was parked. He threw off the cloth covering, and what I saw just hit me - a shining maroon Triumph Speed Twin, a 5 hp twin-cylinder beauty in superb condition. I had dreamed of owning a twin cylinder bike for a long time and found this one simply irresistible, and paid up Rs.2,500 for it (Yes, and not 25,000 !). I used to speed up all round Kalaikunda base, its twin cylinders beating like music to my ears. Someone started calling me 'Speedy' then, and it caught on. Even today, the original Mystere pilots still hail me as 'Speedy'!

I was in my early twenties then, terribly proud of the bike and not shy to show it off! I would time my arrival to work when all the airmen of the squadron would be lined up on the tarmac for roll call. I would ride down and make a steep 180 degree turn to arrive at the parking spot, alight and put it on its side stand and walk off into the crew room, all the while fully aware that the airmen would be watching my 'triumphant' arrival. To make matters more dramatic, I made sure that the final turn was so steep that the bracket on the exhaust pipe scraped on the rough tarmac, making a screeching sound! It gave me a real kick to start the day with dash and style!

Once a pilot from another squadron challenged me to a race against his bike. And so, one evening after the flying was over, we took our bikes on to the runway, which was 2.5km long, to have the race. I won the race easily and clocked a maximum speed of 100mph (160 kmph). The force of the wind was so strong at that speed that it required quite some effort to hold on to the handle.

One day, four of my friends and I got rather late at the bar, and the dining hall had closed up by the time we looked for dinner. We had no choice but to go out to town in search for some food. But the problem was that there was no transport available other than my faithful Triumph! As there was just no question of leaving anyone behind, I decided that all five of us would squeeze on to my bike and have a go. I had to sit on the fuel tank and the last man, Tubby Deviah, was perched precariously on the tail light bracket!. Halfway to town, we spotted a roadside shack with a single bulb lighting up some brass vessels. There was an old woman trying to pack up for the day, with just some remnants of a potato curry and some plain rotis in front of her. She was only too happy to serve us and earn a few more rupees before winding up. We had to democratically share the meagre fare, but enjoyed it. After we finished, we gave her a big tip and returned to our mess, thankful that we did not have to go to bed on an empty stomach !

I had a very good friend in Chini Mehta. We had been together in No.1 Vampire Squadron at Palam, Jamnagar, and Halwara, and then in France for conversion on Mystere, and now in Kalaikunda. He was a great guy, very forthright and uncomplicated! As a young bachelor one does tend to feel lonely at times. It was Chini who filled that gap for me. He was always there as a brother. Though he is no more today, my happy memories of him are very much alive.

xxxxxx

In the summer of 1958, I was deputed as staff-officer to Air Commodore Shivdev Singh, who was appointed as the Air Officer Commanding (AOC) of the newly formed 'No.1 Group'. This group was the precursor to what would later become Eastern Air Command with its headquarters at Tollygunj, Calcutta. I landed up there with my Triumph and luggage, and was put up in an army Mess located within Fort William. This was a Raj-era fort with thick stone walls, and a part of it was used as a mess. It had a rather dungeon-like dark living rooms, and the general atmosphere was just plain grim. The dining hall and bar were, however, well lit and cheerful enough. I would often listen to my collection of Tchaikovsky's symphonies in my room, but eagerly looked forward to weekends, when I would catch a train to Kharagpur and spend time with my squadron mates in Kalaikunda.

My boss, Air Commodore Shivdev Singh, was a kind person and overlooked my slips most magnanimously. On one occasion, while riding my bike to work I got caught in rain and was drenched by the time I reached office. One administrative officer, who loved to pull me down just to feel important, saw me and exclaimed, "Ashok, you can't see the boss in this condition. You better go back and change." Just as he was in the process of giving me a dressing down, and thoroughly enjoying it, in walked the AoC. The moment he saw me, he said "Oh, Ashok *sahib*, you are so drenched, go straight to the heater and dry yourself or you will catch a cold." My tormentor departed in a hurry!

Air Commodore Shivdev Singh was not only a very cool person but also a keen flyer. He would visit Kalaikunda with me in tow and do some flying on the Mystere. He even did a cannon firing sortie at the Balasore range and got some hits on target. Once when he had to attend a meeting in Delhi, we took two Mysteres and flew down from Kalaikunda to Palam in formation. On another occasion, he had to visit all the forward landing strips in the hilly regions in the north-east. We got into a single-engine

Otter aircraft at Jorhat and flew into numerous landing strips, with boss as Captain and self as the co-pilot. It was quite remarkable how he managed to fly so coolly into the short hilly strips and made fairly good landings. I thoroughly enjoyed the rides. He had an even temperament and never lost his shirt. So, in spite of the miserable officers' mess I had to stay in, working with such a boss was a happy experience.

After a few months at this job, I was posted back and stayed with the Mystere squadron for a year, after which I was ordered to report to the Airforce Station Kanpur to join the 'Gnat Handling Flight' which was just being formed there. I was quite thrilled to be selected to fly this latest fighter aircraft, which was about to be inducted into the IAF.

The Smallest Transonic Jet Fighter

Folland Gnat

The Gnat Handling Flight was formed in January 1960 at Kanpur. Initially, there were only three pilots in the flight: Sqn. Ldr.Wollen, who was our boss, Flt.Lt. V.K. Singh and self. Later on, a few other pilots also joined. Our task was flight evaluation of the aircraft before it entered service with the IAF. The Gnat handling flight was a part of Aircraft and Armament Testing Unit (A & ATU), later to be renamed Aircraft & System Testing Establishment (ASTE), now located in Bangalore. From January 1960 to July 1961, we carried out all the operational exercises that the aircraft would be required to carry out in the Air force. These included general handling of the aircraft, aerobatics, formation and tactical flying, dog fights, air to ground weapon delivery, i.e. gun firing, rocket firing and bombing, as well as air-to-air gun firing on a towed target. All the weapons work was done at the Tilpat range near Palam, or at the firing range in Jamnagar.

If I were asked to use one word to describe flying the Gnat, it would have to be 'thrilling'. It was unique, unlike any other fighter aircraft. That does not mean it was easy and altogether pleasant.

The Gnat was designed by the British company, Follands, and was a truly naughty machine, determined to put the pilot in his place! But its taming was a great and rewarding experience. The basic design concept was to have a really small and light fighter aircraft with excellent performance. Small and light made it cheaper to produce and of course, less visible to the enemy. It was just over 6,000 lbs in weight, a mere third of LCA type light fighters, and had an engine of 4,500 lbs thrust. In order to make the aircraft small and light, a number of new concepts were used.

The cockpit was very small with superb visibility. Small pilots felt snug and cosy in it, but for heavier and taller pilots, it was a real squeeze. It had a light-weight ejection seat which did not have ground level ejection capability. A few pilots tragically lost their lives on this account. This was later rectified in the Ajeet, which was an improved Gnat made by HAL.

The pilot's sitting posture was quite unique – his legs being close to horizontal as against the 'dining chair' posture required in most other aircraft. This 'stretched leg' type of posture was a great advantage in providing a high 'g' threshold in tight turns. Due to the near horizontal position of the legs, the downward flow of blood from the head was greatly reduced, thus enabling the pilot to retain his vision at higher values of g, resulting in greater manoeuvring capability in combat situations. Also, its high power to weight ratio enabled it to sustain a steady 7 g in a tight turn at around 400 knots –again a great advantage in combat. It had an exhilarating climb rate of around 10,000 ft per minute which was close to double that of other contemporary fighters. The nose would be way up in the sky and the altimeter would wind up at a fantastic rate.

In order to save weight and avoid complexity, a number of novel features were incorporated in the design: The effect of airbrakes was obtained by partial lowering of the undercarriage so that just the D-doors peeped out into the airflow to increase drag. For this purpose, the undercarriage lever had two positions – first, it would stop at the airbrakes position and further aft movement would lower the undercarriage. There were no separate flaps provided for landing – instead use was made of the ailerons which would droop down to act as flaps, in addition to their primary task of lateral control. What is more, this would happen automatically through a mechanical linkage when the undercarriage moved to the landing position. There was, thus, one single lever to operate airbrakes, undercarriage and flaps. Quite ingenious multiplexing.

The wheel brakes were operated by oil cylinders placed behind the rudder pedals just like in a car. There was no complex brake system as such. The engine start up was achieved by using air pressure from an external ground trolley, thus doing away with the complication of an engine starting system. This also gave a very quick engine start, and was a great help in a 'scramble' situation, where the aircraft has to get airborne as quickly as possible to intercept an intruding enemy aircraft. I held a record for the unbelievably short 'scramble' time of 45 seconds, from the 'command' to get airborne while waiting in a tent nearby, to getting airborne. Most other fighters would need at least a few minutes to get off the ground!

All these innovative devices saved a lot of weight and thus improved the power to weight ratio, resulting in improved performance in air. However, this also resulted in a tightly packed machine, where there was little space between components inside the fuselage and limited access to them. I remember that often they had to call upon one or two slim technicians whose thin arms and hands were needed to reach and dismantle or adjust parts. These personnel had a virtual VIP status in the hangar, as without them you could not proceed. Such were the idiosyncrasies of this machine. But its performance in the air more than made up for the problems it created both for the pilots as well as the ground crew.

The pitch control of the Gnat deserves a special mention. Since the operation of undercarriage to DOWN position also caused landing flaps to be lowered fully, this resulted in a large nose-down trim change and had to be smartly countered by a large movement of stick backwards, along with urgent re-trimming. Likewise, selecting the undercarriage UP after take off caused a *huge* nose up pitching, and the pilot had to push the stick almost fully forward to control it, with some feverish re-trimming! Quite an uncomfortable feature. Anyway, the pilots had to slowly get used to it.

Ejecting

A fighter aircraft provides ample scope for an energetic and exuberant pilot, seeking the thrill of adventure. At that time I was not aware that an aircraft is a sensitive creature and could rap you real hard if you happen to overstep its boundaries, as the following narrative will show.

Prior to joining the Gnat Handling flight, in the Mystere squadron, we used to compete to do a loop at as high an altitude as possible. I remember ending up carrying out a loop, where I reached the top touching 41,000 ft. Since at higher altitudes, the air density drops to very low values, it impairs the aircraft's ability to manoeuvre, thus requiring much greater skill to execute a loop successfully. Hence the challenge!

Since the Gnat had a far superior performance compared to the Mystere aircraft, I thought it should be easier to do such a manoeuvre on it. So, on a crisp winter morning (February 24th, 1960), I got airborne in a Gnat for a handling sortie with the secret intention of executing a loop where I could reach a height greater than 41,000 ft on top, just to beat the Mystere. Unfortunately, the turning performance and control response of Gnat at high altitudes and high Mach number were not as good as on the Mystere. The result was that when I tried this loop, my speed washed off rather rapidly and I got into a spin as I approached the top of the loop at 46,000 ft. The aircraft fell off into a steep nose down attitude and started spinning. It just kept rolling round and round with no let-up. I tried all recommended control inputs to recover but to no avail, and the spin persisted doggedly. This must have carried on for an awfully long time, and when I next looked at the altimeter, we were approaching 10,000 ft. I knew then that there was no hope of recovery and I had to eject and save myself.

The ejection seat of the Gnat was not fully automatic, so I had to first jettison the canopy manually by pulling the jettison lever. I did that, and the canopy flew away, exposing me to the rush of icy cold air. I then reached up above my head to pull the ejection handle, but could not locate it. While I was desperately struggling to reach it, the seat fired by itself (as if by divine intervention!), and I shot out of the aircraft. In a while, the seat separated and fell off. I was hurtling down with my parachute still in the pack, and there was a spiralling motion of my body, which I could not stop. In a short time the parachute opened automatically as it was supposed to, and I felt a hard upward pull as the canopy inflated and stabilized my fall. I looked up and saw the life saving canopy shining in the morning sun, and felt a surge of relief and gratefulness. I took out my map from the flying suit pocket and checked my ground position. I saw that I was near a railway line running south from Lucknow.

After floating for nearly 8 to 10 minutes, I made a reasonable landing on a harvested paddy field covered with stubble. The ground was hard and dry, and there was a strong wind blowing, which kept my parachute canopy inflated. This dragged me some distance, giving me some bruises, till I pressed the quick release box and got separated from the parachute. My back was aching due to the sudden acceleration of the seat, so I spread the silken cloth of the parachute on the ground and lay down on it, face down. Soon, a small village boy appeared looking curious, and I asked him to massage my back. This he did remarkably well and I felt some relief. I could then hear lots of voices from the surrounding fields and soon I had a veritable audience of village folk surrounding me, perplexed by this guy falling from the skies. I got up and was confronted by an old woman who moved her hands over my head and then to her temples to bless me. Coming immediately after my ordeal, I was deeply touched by this gesture of a simple village woman, and thanked her with a grateful heart. I asked the villagers how I could get to the nearest railway station. There was a station called Kankaha some two kilometres away, and the whole procession of villagers led me to it.

I spoke to the station master to send a message to Kanpur to be conveyed to IAF authorities about the incident and that I was safe. I also gave my ground position, with a request to air drop my winter uniform with some money, as I had none. They immediately flew down a two-seater Harvard aircraft, spotted me and dropped a bundle of my clothes with some money in the pocket. I changed into my uniform and bought a ticket to Lucknow on the next train. It was a short journey, and on reaching Lucknow station I was received by virtually a whole platoon of army personnel, including a doctor, who quickly checked me out. Apparently, Army Headquarters had been informed about the accident. They told me that a Dakota aircraft was being positioned at Amausi Airport nearby to pick me up. I was transported to the airport in due course and met my Commanding Officer, Wg. Cdr. Suranjan Das, who had flown down the Dakota along with my colleagues. We reached Kanpur by evening and I was again examined by the IAF doctors. There were only some minor injuries and an aching back, but other than that I was in good shape. My pride had, however, taken a beating. I learnt a big lesson that day: never to take an uncalculated risk with a new machine, without careful planning and risk evaluation – a lesson which held me in good stead in my future test flying career.

In a later incident on the Gnat, a pilot happened to jettison the canopy in the air by mistake, and the ejection seat fired by itself. An investigation revealed that the rubber ejection handle above the pilot's head was not stiff enough and the airflow could bend it backwards and upwards and pull it out, firing the seat. That explained why my seat had fired 'by itself' after I jettisoned the canopy. Divine intervention all right, but through laws of Physics!

The Airforce officers` mess in Kanpur was a barrack type of building modified to function as a mess. There was the standard layout of a lounge, a dining room and, of course a cosy bar. The real attraction was, however, a nice garden in front, with a lawn skirted by numerous flower beds. In spring and summer, there would be a riot of colour with the flowering beds in full bloom. In the evenings numerous chairs and tables would be placed in the lawn, and groups of officers, all in white dress, would gather to sit and chat and have drink together, with the waiter bringing in a continuous supply of snacks. There was a tradition that whoever ordered for drinks would do so for the whole group on that table., and all officers would take their turn. You can imagine what would happen if it was a large group !!

The Gnat Handling Flight was disbanded in June 1961, and I was posted to No. 23 Squadron, the first Gnat squadron of the IAF at Ambala. I was now married and had shifted into the married quarters there. My friend Flt. Lt. VK Singh was the flight commander, and we did a lot of good flying together, squeezing the last ounce of performance out of the Gnat.

My happy association with VK, was however, not destined to last for long. In January 1962, the squadron was to put up two 'box' formations of four aircraft each for the forthcoming Republic Day flypast at Delhi. Sqn. Ldr. Mally Wollen, by then our Commanding Officer, was to lead the first box, followed by self, leading the second box. VK being the deputy leader of the whole formation was in the first box with Mally. We used to take off from Ambala, do the fly-past rehearsal over Palam airfield, and fly back to Ambala. On 24th January, after we had completed our practice fly-past over Palam, and were setting course for Ambala, VK peeled off to land at Palam to attend a debriefing there. When we landed back at Ambala, we were told that VK's aircraft had collided with a Vampire aircraft flown by Wg. Cdr. Zafar Shah (who was the officer in charge of flying at Palam). This happened when both were in the process of joining circuit for landing at Palam, and both pilots had been killed. It was a rude shock to all of us, and a pall of gloom descended on the squadron. I lost a good friend and would miss him deeply. But such is the business of fighter flying. I have encountered such sad and painful occasions far too regularly during my nearly four decades of fighter flying with IAF and HAL. I have lost over a dozen good friends this way. The price is a bit too heavy for the thrill of flying fighters. But destiny had led us there, and we had to bear the penalties as well.

In September 1961, we were blessed with our first child, a daughter. At that time I was in the midst of my promotion exams, and to my eternal regret, could not be present at the hospital. It was a great joy to see the small bundle next morning, neatly tucked beside my wife Meera.

In May 1962, I was posted as Flight Commander to the newly formed No.2 Gnat Squadron, also at Ambala. It was my responsibility to convert a bunch of young Toofani pilots onto the Gnat aircraft. Since the Gnat did not have a trainer aircraft, the Squadron had been allotted two Hunter MK 66, (a two-seater aircraft) to familiarize the Toofani pilots with powered flight controls and high speed flying, before launching them off on the Gnat. Our Squadron commander was Sqn. Ldr. J. N. Jatar, who had already flown the Gnat. Apart from the two of us, nobody else had any experience on the Gnat.

I carried out training flights on the Hunter with each of the Toofani pilots to give them some experience on powered flight controls. But the Hunter was a gentleman's aircraft, whereas the Gnat was like a spoilt brat – extremely touchy on controls and with its terrific acceleration, it could really run away from the pilot. The jump from Hunter to Gnat was not that easy, but detailed briefing and a cautious approach enabled all the pilots to do their solos on the aircraft in reasonable time. I felt greatly relieved when all of them converted safely. In due course, they came to love the Gnat for its energy and agility. My pleasant time in the squadron came to an end when, in Dec 1962, I was selected for the Test Pilot's course in the UK.

Test Pilot Training

Empire Test Pilots' School (ETPS), Farnborough, UK

I was to attend the Empire Test Pilots' School (ETPS) in Farnborough, UK in February 1963 along with my good friend Flt. Lt. Omi Mathur, who had been my roommate at Kalaikunda. Both of us were fighter pilots and had no experience of transport or bomber aircraft. Since the course at ETPS involved flying all types of aircraft, the IAF considered it prudent to give us some experience on transport and bomber aircraft, prior to attending the course.

The very first transport aircraft that we flew was the Avro (HS748), twin-engine turbo-prop aircraft, which had a 44 seat capacity. At that time in late 1962, there was only one Avro aircraft in the country – and it was the first aircraft produced by Aircraft Manufacturing Depot (AMD), Kanpur (later to become HAL Kanpur). Sqn. Ldr. Kapil Bhargava was the Chief Test Pilot at AMD. He took us up for a brief familiarization flight where both Omi Mathur and I handled the controls and carried out some landings. It was a short bit of familiarization with a transport aircraft, but was most useful. Flying with a celebrated Test Pilot like Kapil Bhargava was itself a treat.

We then went to Palam to fly the good old DC-3 Dakota. This was a vintage twin piston engine transport aircraft, and we had to get familiar again with mixture control, magneto and the like. Even though we had to do just a few flights to get a general feel of transport aircraft, our instructors there, transport kingpins, insisted on us carrying out three- point landings – where all three wheels of the aircraft have to touch the runway surface at the same time. This necessarily involved landing at very low speeds, just short of a stall, when the aircraft would sink rapidly prior to touching down. You had to judge your height very accurately; otherwise you could thump down hard on the runway. On the other hand, if you did not have the correct nose up attitude at touch down, you could go bouncing like a kangaroo. We were not at all pleased with their insistence on three-point landings.

For our short familiarization, the easier landing with the two main wheels touching down first would have sufficed, but we had to do as told, as it was the only way to be cleared for solo flights. With concerted practice, we managed to show some reasonable three-point landings, and were cleared for solo. We both did a few flights together, acting alternately as Captain and co-pilot, and enjoyed it. The Dak, as the Dakota was popularly called, was a great machine at that level of technology. The manual flight controls were beautifully harmonized, and the engine response was excellent, as with most piston engines. It had a primitive auto pilot, and some basic instruments. It was undoubtedly a great transport aircraft of its time and its worldwide popularity was well deserved.

We then went to Agra to fly the Canberra bomber. Our instructor there was my old friend and course mate, Qaisar Ali. He was a cool instructor and gave us some fine tips on flying the Canberra. Both Omi Mathur and I did our solos and had a satisfying exposure to this medium Jet bomber.

In view of the foreign exchange limitations following the Chinese invasion of 1962, the government cleared only one pilot to attend the Test Pilots course at ETPS. Being senior to Flt.Lt. Omi Mathur, I was selected to go first. I could not take my family with me as the government did not clear adequate allowance on account of the same foreign exchange limitations.

I arrived in London in early February 1963 by an Air India flight, and reported to the Indian High Commission for briefing and other formalities. This took a few days, after which I caught a train to Farnborough and arrived at the railway station, a quiet, almost deserted place. A solitary cab parked outside took me to ETPS Mess and I was allotted a room in the annexe. It was a small cosy room with a bed, a writing table and chair, and a deep upholstered easy chair. It had a heating system based on hot water circulation through a grill comprising pipes. It was a severe winter that year, and the first thing I did after entering the room was to warm my feet. It was a procedure I would adopt very often during those winter months, when I returned in the evening, quite exhausted after some strenuous flights.

Test Pilot Training

The first problem I faced was to have the mess staff arrange vegetarian food for me, as I was the lone vegetarian and also the only Asian. For quite some time I managed on salads and egg dishes, good bread, butter and cheese and a generous helping of dessert. But I missed proper Indian food a lot and so whenever I later visited London, I would head for an Indian restaurant and eat to my heart's content.

The ETPS was commanded by Gp. Capt. Watts of the Royal Airforce – a somewhat elderly looking gentleman; and the Chief Test Flying Instructor was Wg. Cdr. Hubbard, an energetic and vigorous sort of person. Other instructors were Lt. Cdr. Humphreys of the Royal Navy, Sqn. Ldr. Mellors and Eddie Rigg of the Royal air force. Humphreys and Mellors were gentle souls but Eddie was the opposite.

There were three semesters in the course and I had to work one semester each with the three instructors. The daily schedule comprised two-morning classes, mostly on aerodynamics and flight test techniques, and thereafter, the whole day was devoted to flying. We had a reasonable spread of aircraft types – Chipmunk, Piston Provost, Devon, Hunter MK 1 and MK 4, Meteor 7, Vampire T.II, Canberra B2 and T4, and Viscount - a four-engine turboprop transport aircraft. Towards the end of the course, we also got to fly the Scimitar, a robust transonic naval fighter.

The first few weeks were spent in trying to familiarize ourselves with the different types of aircraft. We were given the Pilot manuals for each and where possible, a few dual checks, to send us on our first solo flights. Thereafter, one's name would be put up on a huge black board every afternoon, indicating the type of aircraft one was programmed to fly the next day. We would need to hurriedly go through the relevant pilot manual to be ready for the flight next morning. There was little supervision as such, and we were left to manage things on our own. To top it all, nobody would advise us if the weather was suitable for flying – you had to refer to the met report and decide for yourself. I watched what the other pilots were doing and tried to follow their example. It would often be cloudy and rainy, but most of the pilots there were used to that sort of weather and would get airborne. I was the only Asian pilot, used to sunny weather, and so getting airborne in rainy weather in a machine that I was not familiar with, definitely caused me some anxiety. But the air traffic and radar controllers were excellent, and in due course, I was happy flying in such weather and carrying out radar assisted landings in the rain. My only concern was the ominous possibility of radio failure. In the case of really bad weather; without radio, no guidance was possible from ground controllers. As luck would have it, there was not a single case of radio failure, for which we were truly grateful to the maintenance staff.

The very first flight I went up for was in a Chipmunk, a light piston engine trainer aircraft. It was mid-February and cold as hell, with snow blanketing the countryside. I carried out a normal flight in the allotted area and was returning to base, but I could not locate the runway - a tiny black line among many other black lines like roads and railway lines, in that great white snowy expanse. The Air Traffic Control had to guide me on to the runway, which I embarrassingly spotted only when right overhead. The Chipmunk itself was a sweet machine and had good flying qualities. I could soon ensure good three-point landings, and also carried out a full spinning programme on it.

I was familiar with the Vampire trainer aircraft, as we had it in our air force. We had the Meteor MK 7, a two-seat twin-engine jet fighter. It was of World War II vintage, but a powerful machine and most delightful to fly. It was also used for instrument ratings of pilots. The two engines were podded- one on each wing, clearly detracting from the typical fighter aircraft look. But they provided excellent acceleration and climb performance. We carried out some instrument calibration exercises on it. One peculiar and unfortunate characteristic of this aircraft was that when flying on single engine, the use of airbrakes with undercarriage down, could cause you to lose control of the aircraft. The airbrakes were large panels which would pop up over the wing root, and could apparently cause major disturbance to the airflow over the tail under certain conditions of flight. This would seriously impair the effectiveness of the elevator. Somehow, this problem would occur only when flying on single engine with undercarriage down and not when operating normally on two engines. We were all warned never to use airbrakes when flying on single engine with the undercarriage down.

Unfortunately, precisely this phenomenon trapped my friend Flt. Lt. Omi Mathur, who attended a later course. While practicing single engine landings, he by mistake, used airbrakes when on circuit with undercarriage down, and the aircraft nose-dived into the ground and he was killed. I was deeply pained to lose a good friend so avoidably. We had been in France together for conversion on Mystere IV aircraft, and were later roommates in Kalaikunda on the first Mystere IV squadron. He was a good natured and gentlemanly officer. But fate has its own unfathomable reasons, and often takes away the best early on.

Test Pilot Training

Then we had the Hunter MK 7 (two-seater) and the Hunter MK 4 (single seater) fighter aircraft, which were generally similar to the Hunter aircraft of the Indian Airforce, but were older models. The most significant difference was that these older models did not have wing leading edge extensions near the wing tip region. As a result, the wing tip area would stall earlier than the rest of the wing at high angles of attack, thus causing the centre of lift to move inwards. On an aircraft with swept back wings, inward movement of lift amounts to forward movement in relation to the fuselage. This would cause the nose of the aircraft to pitch -up abruptly. One would often need to apply full forward stick to recover from such a condition. It could even lead you into a spin. This phenomenon was common to the Mystere aircraft also which we had in our IAF. But on the Hunter, the manufacturers carried out a major modification to provide leading edge extension near the wing tips, which cured the problem. The Hunter aircraft in service with IAF were all modified machines, so the pilots did not get a surprise pitch up.

Although, both Hunter MK 7 and MK 4 were unmodified, they were, nevertheless, lovely flying machines with unmatched elegance both in looks and character, and I carried out some challenging tests on them.

One notable exercise I carried out with my instructor on the two-seat Hunter MK 7 was an inverted spin triggered by 'inertia coupling'. It was the first time I experienced this not-well-understood phenomenon. 'Inertia coupling' – also called 'roll-yaw' coupling- is a phenomenon peculiar to high performance fighters, which have most of their mass concentrated on the fuselage, as compared to the wings; the latter being rather thin for high speed flight. When such an aircraft is rolled continuously and rapidly, the predominant inertia axis (in this case, the fuselage line) tends to gradually shift outwards causing a barrelling effect, resulting in a sideslip to set in –where the relative airflow starts coming on to the aircraft from one side, and not along the fuselage line. The sideslip angle would progressively increase as the rolling continues, subjecting the vertical fin to higher and higher side loads. It could even reach its structural limit and finally break off, causing an uncontrolled spin into the ground. Such was the fate of some pioneering test pilots who first attempted rapid and sustained rolling of their high speed fighter aircraft. At that time, (in the late 40's I think), this phenomenon was not fully understood. In many modern high speed fighter aircraft, continuous rolling manoeuvres are forbidden because of the risk of getting into inertia coupling.

On the Hunter MK 7, my instructor showed me this phenomenon at a height of 40,000 ft, and at a low speed, where the air loads are well within structural limits of the aircraft. At that height, we stabilized in level flight at a low speed of 160 knots. My instructor asked me to start rolling to left with full stick deflection in order to get a high rate of roll as quickly as possible. As we completed some three to four rolls, the roll rate became really rapid and the rudder abruptly deflected to full right position because of the large induced sideslip. In an instant, we were in an inverted spin. It was a smooth spin but rather disorienting as we were inverted. After a few turns, opposite rudder and aft movement of stick got us out of the spin reasonably fast. I carried out one or two more such spins to get a hang of it. It was a unique experience for me and most pilots would never have had such an experience in their flying careers. An inertia coupling resulting in an inverted spin is a unique phenomenon on the Hunter. This is so on account of the rudder on this aircraft not being hydraulically powered and hence deflecting due to high side-slip angle and triggering the spin.

The next aircraft I moved on to was the Piston Provost. This was a two-seater trainer aircraft and quite a delight to fly. It had two side by side seats and performed well for a piston engine light machine. I was given an exercise to evaluate its takeoff and landing characteristics and had a great time with it. By the time I finished my evaluation in some 5 to 6 flights I could manage really smooth three point landings. Once I was asked to take this aircraft to a nearby airfield to drop someone. When I came in for landing at this airfield, the wind was some 15 knots right down the runway and the landing I managed was one of the best I have carried out. We literally did not know when we had touched down. At that time I did not anticipate any negative thrills on this gentlemanly machine, but I was in for a surprise.

As part of the course, I was to carry out a timed ceiling climb on this aircraft. This test involves climbing the aircraft virtually as high as it would go, and in the climb noting all the engine parameters and altitude attained etc every 30 seconds. Since the aircraft was not pressurized and could well climb to around 25,000 ft, I had to carry an oxygen bottle and manage the low pressure and sub-zero temperatures to the best of my abilities. I climbed on a westerly heading, maintaining accurate speed and noting down numerous parameters. I was madly busy and thus had no time for navigation checks or any such activity. Finally, I finished the climb at 24,000 ft, royally chilled and exhausted.

When I took stock of my ground position, I noticed that I was over the Bristol Channel, far far away from Farnborough. Apparently there was a strong wind blowing me westward. I immediately turned back towards base and got down to checking all the systems in the cockpit, for which I had had no time during the climb. I was shocked to find my fuel contents very low, contrary to my calculation. I immediately called up Boscombe Downe air base, which was the closest airfield, and requested a radar recovery and an emergency landing. Boscombe Downe radar immediately gave me a course to steer and confirmed that they would place me on the final approach without delay; which they did. On the long final approach, my fuel gauge was reading close to zero and I wondered if I would need to land short of the runway on one of the neat farms. By the time I came over the runway, the gauge had dropped to below zero and I expected my engine to cut any moment. But luck was in my favour and I managed to land and even taxied up to the parking area and switched off.

After getting out of the aircraft, I asked the ground crew to top up the tanks. When I checked the quantity of fuel put in, it was exactly same as the capacity of the tank! In other words, I had used up the last few drops of fuel by the time I switched off. It was a fantastic coincidence and a real lucky day for me. From there to my home base at Farnborough was a short flight of some 30 minutes. After landing there, when I explained the reason for my diversion as fuel shortage, I was told that on this aircraft there was a possibility of fuel siphoning off to the atmosphere through one of the air vents in the wing tanks. This explained the rapid and undetected reduction in the fuel gauge reading towards the latter part of the flight. I was lucky not to have ended up on some field short of the runway with damage to my aircraft, and possibly to my bones, if not worse.

We had two Canberra Jet bombers on our course - the T4 trainer and the B2 bomber. I had briefly flown the T4 and B58 versions in India, and was somewhat familiar with the machines. I carried out stall tests and single engine controllability tests on these aircraft. However, what I remember more vividly is the fact that whenever I was slotted for a flight on the Canberra, the weather would turn deeply cloudy with heavy rain, and more often than not, I would need to depend entirely on the Radar controller at Farnborough to place me on the final approach for landing. The cloud base would be very low with incessant rain, making it really dark, and in winter the sunset was very early, around 4 pm. Under these conditions, I could just about make out the runway lights as I broke cloud.

After a long and stressful flight in such weather, the appearance of those two rows of runway lights was a most welcome sight!

We also had the twin piston engine commuter aircraft called Dove (or Devon). This was used mostly for tests requiring different centre of gravity (CG) positions, to establish longitudinal stability margins. To get the required centre of gravity, appropriate ballast weights would be placed at different points inside the cabin. The Devon itself was a sweet little machine, and had one of the most comfortable cockpits. In later years, when I was posted as a test pilot in Kanpur, I would often be called upon to fly this aircraft to ferry some senior IAF officers from one place to another, and I rather enjoyed those trips.

The four-engine turbo-prop aircraft Viscount, was a proper airliner, in service with Indian Airlines. It was a unique experience to carry out some test flights on this aircraft. My instructor gave me three dual sorties before sending me solo, with a flight engineer as my co-pilot! Thereafter, I carried out a number of flights for auto pilot assessment. I never thought that I would be one day flying a four-engine transport aircraft, and that too without a fuss. In ETPS, they believed in exposing the trainee test pilots to such challenges with only the minimum of supervision. At the end of the course, we had a feedback session where all the students expressed their unanimous opinion that they took too many chances with us. Their response was that only through such tough challenges did they produce confident and capable test pilots. It spoke volumes about their approach to test flying. I think it was an accurate statement.

By the time we graduated as test pilots, we really had the confidence to fly any type of aircraft – in fact, there was a pressing desire to get one's hands on to as many different types of aircraft as possible – a hankering which never left me all through my test flying career. I realized that the greater the challenge, the greater is the reward in overcoming it, and greater the confidence acquired.

I was also one of the few students who were given some flying experience on a transonic Naval fighter called Scimitar. This was a robust single-seat aircraft with a really tough landing gear to take the shock of hard thumping landings that naval aircraft need to make on an aircraft carrier. It had two powerful Avon engines imbedded in the fuselage, and landing flaps with boundary layer control (also called blown flaps). This system blows high pressure air from the engine compressor on to the top surfaces of the flaps to increase lift. This enables the aircraft to come in for landing

Test Pilot Training

at lower speeds, a crucial requirement for landing safely on the short deck of an aircraft carrier. These days, some modern fighter aircraft have such a facility on them, but back in 1963, it was still a novelty. When I went for my first flight on the Scimitar, the cloud base was just 500 ft above ground and it was a total overcast. I had to get onto instrument flying immediately on getting airborne and remain on it till I finally broke cloud at 30,000 ft.

The climbing speed of the Scimitar was 500 knots and 0.9 Mach at higher altitudes; the highest climbing speed I have come across on any aircraft, except for the supersonic climb on MiG 21, where you lunge upwards at 1.8 Mach. For landing the Scimitar, we were briefed to just let the aircraft thump down on the runway without a flare. Just as they do for deck landings. But being an *Airforce* pilot, and somewhat more sensitive about how we treat our aircraft, I did not have the heart to thump such a monster of an aircraft hard on to the runway. I carried out many 'touch and go' landings giving a small burst of engine power just before touchdown. I found that a soft landing was not that difficult to achieve. This went against the briefing, but my instructor was mighty pleased, and simply pulled my leg saying that on a carrier deck, I would find myself in the sea!

In addition to flying various types of aircraft on the course, we were also offered some experience on gliders, i.e. sailplanes, over the weekends during summer months, and I enjoyed it greatly. We had two types of gliders – one was the two-seater T-21B Slingsby, and the other one was a single seat Gruno Baby. We used the Chipmunk for glider towing and would get towed up to some 3,000 to 4,000 ft when we would release the tow and start looking for some air currents which could take us up further. If we were lucky to catch one, we would go further and further up and stay afloat for almost an hour. It was great fun.

I had a great friend in Lt. Cdr. Dave Eagles of the Royal Navy, who was also on the course. He was married and lived with his wife in a picturesque house in a nearby village called Camberley. Some weekends he would call me over for lunch and his wife would graciously make a special vegetable pie for me, which I relished. Dave used to tend honey bees and had a number of large wooden pigeon holes for them to nest in. He was also quite knowledgeable about them and showed me how these bees had a unique system of communication to indicate the location of a new found source of nectar. On returning to the hive, the bee would crawl nearby, describing a perfect isosceles triangle, the apex of which would point in the direction of the source, and the height of the triangle would be a scaled down measure of the distance to it! And we humans think we are the only intelligent beings on this planet!

A while after graduating as a Test Pilot, Dave Eagles carried out the first flight of the EAP, the forerunner to the much vaunted Eurofighter. Later, he became the Chief Test Pilot and Executive Director of British Aerospace. As luck would have it, I too held precisely these two designations at Hindustan Aeronautics, prior to my retirement. A happy coincidence for two good friends.

There were three Americans on the course - one was Captain Pogue from the U.S. Air force. He later became an astronaut and stayed at the international space station for some length of time. The other two were Lt. Cdr. Jerry Skyrud and Lt. Disher from the US Navy. Jerry was the senior-most officer on the course, and was thus appointed as the course-in-charge. He was particularly friendly with me. I remember one occasion when he called the whole course for a party at his house. It was a rollicking party and half way through, he called for a toast and sang, "Happy Birthday to you, Ash!"That was for me; it was 13th October 1963, my 29th birthday, and I had thought no one knew about it. Not only that, everyone came out with a gift for the occasion. Somehow, a group engaged in flying together almost always bonds very well.

There was also a pilot from the Australian Airforce on the course. But soon after our course started, he was involved in an accident while carrying out a touch-and-go landing on a Canberra aircraft. As he opened full throttle to take off again (after touch-down), one of the engines failed, and the aircraft swung viciously into a ground loop and went off the runway, causing much damage to the machine; luckily the crew were not hurt. Consequently, he was suspended from the course and sadly, had to pack up and return home. The Canberra engine did not have an acceleration control which regulates the fuel flow during throttle opening to avoid over-fuelling and consequent surge which could result in a flameout. On such engines, the only way to avoid a flameout was to open throttle very gently. Apparently, he was too fast on the throttle, probably not used to operating such engines. His was the only suspension on the course.

Before the end of the course, and before it got too cold, ETPS offered a parachuting experience to all the students, on a voluntary basis. I readily volunteered for it; since I had earlier ejected from a Gnat and had some parachuting experience. I also wanted to repeat it in more friendly circumstances, as a sport. Moreover, we were to jump off over the sea, which would be a new experience anyway. We were to fly in a Beverly transport aircraft and jump off from 3,000 ft over a sea channel called The Solent, between the south coast of England (near Southampton), and the Isle of Wight. We took off from Farnborough on a clear sunny day and arrived at the south coast. We were grouped into batches of three, all three being cleared to jump one after the other with a gap of two seconds. There were three motor boats positioned for the purpose of picking up the parachutists, one for each parachutist, to enable quick recovery. We had to wear safety vests to assist in floating and were briefed to release the parachute just before hitting water, to ensure that it did not collapse on top of you and choke you. A necessary precaution.

As per the briefing, we jumped from the rear door of the aircraft. I was the third in my batch of three. The static line anchored to the aircraft snapped the parachute open soon after the jump, and we floated down merrily one on top of the other and close enough to shout and talk to one another. As we neared the water, I was a bit late in releasing the parachute and hit the water first. But fortunately, a mild breeze drifted the parachute to a safe distance and my motor boat reached me very quickly. It was quite cold in the water, and the moment I boarded the boat, a big bath towel was handed to me. I dried off and changed into dry clothes which had been packed and kept on the designated boat. It was nice and warm in the bright sun, the sparkling sea and clear blue sky adding to the charm.

Towards the end of October 1963, we had completed all our test flying exercises and were allotted one aircraft each for a comprehensive evaluation in all its varied aspects. A detailed preview report was to be submitted at the end of the evaluation. We were allowed six hours of flying each, and a month's time to complete the task. During this period there was no other work to be done and we were left to plan and complete the evaluation entirely on our own. I was allotted the single seat twin-engine Meteor MK 8 fighter. This aircraft was very different to the two seat MK 7 which I had flown there. It was a challenging task to complete the evaluation economically within just six hours of flying, including night flying. The whole object was to apply all that we had learnt about test flying techniques during the course, and to produce a comprehensive report describing the aircraft's characteristics in detail. There was also an award for the best preview report. It was akin to a thesis for graduating as a Test Pilot.

I greatly enjoyed flying the Meteor MK 8 and found it to be quite different and far superior to the two-seat Meteor Trainer in handling characteristics, as well as in performance. By the end of November, I compiled a fat Preview Report in two volumes, which I submitted with a great sense of relief.

The final day soon arrived for the graduation ceremony. There was to be a formal dinner, where numerous aviation stalwarts were invited, many of them well known and celebrated Test Pilots from the Aviation industry. Four awards were slated to be given: the McKenna Trophy for the pilot who tops the course and one for the Runner-Up. Then there was the Edwards Award for best progress on the course and a Hawker Hunter Trophy for the best Preview Report. No one was told who would get the awards; it was a close secret. When the party started and everyone was busy having cocktails in the lounge, some guesses were being made in whispers about the possible winners, but no one knew anything for sure. My pal Mike Adams of the RAF, who was standing quite far from me, gave me an emphatic, elevated thumbs-up when our eyes met. I wondered what he could have meant, and thought of the possibility that he may have seen our instructor's remarks on my preview report. He was in the habit of checking other pilots` reports from time to time, and was rather well informed about the goings on behind the scenes.

We were all in the formal uniforms of our respective Service, and the whole atmosphere was sort of celebratory. In due course, a bell was sounded for us to shift into the dining hall to occupy our allotted seats. The layout of the tables was in accordance with that of a formal dining-in night, as is common in the Services. The U.K. minister for Aviation was to preside over the event. The five-course dinner was served and partaken of in the usual manner, and we were all served coffee. Some speeches were then made and the course report read out.

It was then time for the awards to be announced and presented. The first one was, of course, the McKenna trophy for the top student. This went to my pal, Mike Adams. That was a popular expectation. The runners-up trophy went to John Farley, who later on did a lot of pioneering testing on the Harrier Jump Jet. The next announcement was for the Edward's Award for the best progress on the course, and I was astonished when my name was called out. I was thrilled to get the award from the minister and got back to my seat amidst a lot of applause. The next award for the best Preview Report was then announced, and I heard my name being called out again. Though I was pleased with my preview flying and report, I never expected the award for it. I was, of course, thrilled to go up again to be greeted by the minister. It was a tough and challenging course and I was happy and proud to have done well. The graduation certificate authorized

Test Pilot Training

us to flight test any fixed wing prototype aircraft of any design; something I greatly valued. It was a culmination of a secret wish I had harboured during my early years in the IAF, and I was grateful that it had materialized.

After completion of the Test Pilots' course at ETPS in Dec.1963, I was attached to the then British Aircraft Corporation (later, a part of British Aerospace) for some test flying experience with their industry. It was for a duration of six months, most of which I spent at their Flight Test Centre at Wisley, where Design, Development and flight testing of big jets was done. I would have been quite happy to return to India as I missed my wife and little daughter deeply, but it was also a rare opportunity to fly some new aircraft of the British aviation industry and I wanted to make the most of it.

The Flight Test Centre at Wisley was fully occupied with development flying of two types of aircraft at that time – the four engine VC-10 airliner and the smaller two-engine commuter jet BAC 1-11. The latter aircraft was one of the earliest jets to have its two engines mounted on the rear end of the fuselage, one on each side. This necessitated a T-tail configuration, which meant a tall fin with the elevators positioned right on top of it, since the lower space was occupied by the engines. This configuration had resulted in an unfortunate crash which occurred a little before our ETPS course started, killing all the flight crew. The crash site was in our local flying area at Farnborough. We could see it from the air, and could actually make out the plan view of the aircraft as it had hit the ground in a flat attitude with little forward speed. Investigations into the accident had concluded that it had got into what is called a 'deep stall' and that the elevator power was not sufficient to recover it from that attitude. This was later established as a phenomenon peculiar to T-tail configuration where at high angles of attack, the elevator comes into the wake of disturbed air-flow from the wings and forward parts of the aircraft, thus reducing its effectiveness. By the time I flew the BAC 1-11 on a few flights, they had increased the elevator power and also provided an automatic stick pusher which would pitch the aircraft nose down at a predetermined angle of attack, thus preventing it from getting into a deep stall. Once these problems were overcome, the aircraft proved to be a winner, and many airlines took to it eagerly.

The VC-10 was a proper intercontinental airliner and was slightly bigger and much more sophisticated than the celebrated Boeing 707. It had four jet engines located at the rear fuselage, two on each side, and thus also had a T-tail. But various improvements in design protected it from entering a deep stall. I got a lot of ground training on the aircraft's systems and other characteristics and procedures before starting to fly it, first as a co-pilot and then a few flights from the Captain's seat. It was a finely designed and engineered machine with lots of power and excellent powered flight controls. It had a very long fuselage, and the wings were located rather far back, and so also its main undercarriage. The runway at Wisley was a long strip, without any taxi tracks feeding its ends. We had to enter the runway midway and backtrack to the appropriate dumbbell (i.e. a runway end), and turn around to line up for takeoff.

Because the cockpit was way ahead of the main wheels, it was not possible for the pilots to visualize the path the main wheels would describe while turning around at the dumbbell for takeoff. To ensure that the wheels stayed on the concrete surface, and did not go off on to the grass, an ingenious method had been worked out. They had marked a white line on the ground on which the pilot had to accurately keep the cockpit throughout the turnaround, to ensure that the wheels remained on the concrete. The line would take the cockpit way off the concrete and well onto the grass, a somewhat uncomfortable feeling in the beginning. But, through recourse to some accurate geometry, it was ensured that all three wheels stayed on the runway as long as the cockpit was kept accurately over the white line! The nose wheel steering was with a wheel on the side and had excellent feel – same with the pedal wheel brakes. It was a smooth ride and a pleasure to taxy. Take-off acceleration was very good and it got off the runway smoothly and into a steep climb at regulation 160 knots. The engines were very responsive and the cabin was really silent as the engines were way behind.

We would often climb to 40,000 ft or thereabouts in a reasonably short time for various tests. On one test, I was to dive the aircraft to the limit test Mach number of 0.95 Mach. I was in a reasonably shallow dive to ensure I did not exceed 0.95 Mach. But as we approached that speed, the mach-meter jumped to a little over Mach 1.0. Oops! we had gone supersonic on this huge four-engine jetliner. I promptly throttled back and eased her out of the dive with no difficulty. It was a smooth ride all the way, without any significant pitching or any other adverse response. Good aerodynamics, indeed.

As with all big jets, in the landing attitude with the nose up, the pilots were on a high perch at the point of touch down, making it that much more difficult to judge the height accurately. However, after a little practice, I got the hang of the perspective required for a good touchdown, and was

Test Pilot Training

even able to manage some silky landings. I did have some problem though, in lining up on the final approach, as the aircraft sat tight where it was put. Making fine course corrections required some effort and anticipation, as was true of all big and heavy aircraft. But, as I was essentially a fighter pilot, I was used to course corrections with a flick of the wrist. Wheeling a lumbering jetliner to line up with the runway centreline accurately, did cause me to struggle a bit initially, but I got the hang of it soon enough. Altogether, it was a great experience flying the VC-10, a real novelty for me.

John Cochran was the British pilot with whom I did most of my flying on the VC-10. He was to later carry out development flying on the Concorde supersonic airliner. The Chief Test Pilot at BAC Wisley, was a stocky chain-smoking bachelor called Brian Trubshaw. He too had later got on to the Concorde development flights, along with his French counterpart. He was a celebrated Test Pilot, and a rather reserved and tense sort of person. I flew a few flights with him as a co-pilot during stall tests on the VC-10. In view of the earlier accident on the BAC 1-11 due to deep stall, we had to carry parachutes, in case of a need to bale-out. However, we had no problem with the stalls as the elevators were powerful enough to ensure recovery.

While at BAC, Wisley, I sat in an office which I shared with a young communication pilot by the name of Eric Bucklowe. He was a relaxed and friendly person, and we were good company to each other. He used to fly a commuter shuttle service between Wisley and Filton, near Bristol. I often flew with him as a co-pilot one way, and Captain the other way. Two types of commuter aircraft were there at Wisley – one was a Devon and another a small four piston- engine aircraft called Heron. It was more or less like a four engine Devon. I had a great time flying these machines, often in really bad weather, and so became fairly adept at instrument landings.

By July 1964 my deputation with British Aircraft Corporation came to an end. It was now time to go home. Cheers !

Early Years as a Test Pilot

AIR FORCE, KANPUR

Auster IX, Harvard, Otter, Vampire, Toofani, Mystere, Hunter & Ilyushin 14

I returned to India and reported to Air Headquarters, where I was informed about my posting to No.1 BRD (Base Repair Depot) at Kanpur. I also got my promotion to the rank of Squadron Leader. I then proceeded on some leave to join my wife and daughter at Bhopal. My daughter who had been just over a year old when I left for the UK, was now nearly three years old. It was a delight to be re-united with my family and to get to make friends afresh with my daughter. In September'64, I arrived in Kanpur and looked forward to engaging with the wonderful line-up of aeroplanes there.

The flying unit at No.1 BRD was called Aircraft Testing & Ferry Flight (AT&FF), and was located in a small independent building standing somewhat aloof from the line-up of huge hangars which housed technical facilities. The building had a little garden and a kitchenette to provide for tea and nimboo pani etc to pilots returning from flights. It had a pleasant and peaceful atmosphere, well away from the crowded and noisy hangars.

For a freshly graduated Test Pilot, the line up of aircraft which came up for flight tests at No. 1 BRD, was really the best thing that could have happened – Vampires, Toofanis, Mysteres and Hunters amongst jet fighters, and Auster, Harvard and Otter in the piston engine, light aircraft category. Occasionally, a few other types of aircraft would also be offered. But the bulk of flying was on fighters, completely to my taste. Most days I would fly two or three aircraft and revel in it. It was an intense grounding into test flying, and I loved it every bit.

Most of the aircraft there had come for major overhaul – to be fully stripped and then re-assembled after repairs and replacements of parts. A fresh overhauled engine would be fitted. As such, they were virtually like new aircraft, and hence would need to be thoroughly tested in the air. Numerous defects would be revealed in the test flights which would need rectification, followed by further flights to confirm satisfactory performance. This whole process offered an excellent opportunity for learning the nitty-gritty of test flying, and I felt greatly privileged to have this experience so soon after my entry into this exciting world. It helped provide a solid foundation to my test flying career.

AUSTER

The Auster IX was a light single piston engine aircraft of old design with side by side seating and was used mostly for Air observation purposes by the army. I remember the awkward positioning of the throttle in the centre of the instrument panel, much like the choke lever in old cars. Pushing it in, increased the power, and pulling it out brought it to idle. Since the captain's seat was on the left, the throttle had to be operated by his right hand, which meant holding the stick with the left hand. In my military flying training, we always had the throttle lever on the left, so that the stick could be held in the right hand at all times, as with all fighter aircraft. I never felt comfortable manipulating the stick with the left hand, especially during landing, where greater precision is needed. Thus, I had to deftly shift my right hand from the throttle to the stick in the last moments before landing, after the throttle had been pulled back fully to idle. This was fine as long as the landing was good. But if the landing was a bit rough or bouncy, I needed to use the throttle to stabilize the situation, for which I had to shift my right hand from the stick back to the throttle and move my left hand back to the stick, at such a critical point during landing. Not the best of things to do. Anyway, such was the design and one had to live with it. If in place of a straight stick as in the Auster, we had a half-wheel type of control stick, as in transport aircraft, the situation would have been quite acceptable. I have not been able to figure out why and how the shape of the control column (or stick) should make such a profound difference. May be some ergonomics expert could provide the answer.

On one occasion we had an Auster aircraft which gave severe engine vibrations in the air. Numerous rectifications were attempted to fix the problem but the vibrations persisted. The technical staff were at their wits end, when some smart guy suggested that probably the pilots were being too fussy. After all, all engines vibrate. So, the Station Commander, Air Commodore Nayyar of the Technical branch, himself decided to check first-hand how bad the situation was. The thing to note here is that the severity of vibrations cannot be accurately measured on ground, as contact with the ground through the wheels dampens the vibrations considerably. In the air it shows its true colours.

So, I got airborne with Air Commodore Nayyar in the right seat. As soon as we got airborne, the full force of vibrations broke out, and apparently, gave quite a fright to the Station Commander. He asked me to land back immediately. Thereafter, the pilot's observations were never questioned. The engine was replaced with a new one to clear the aircraft.

OTTER

The single-engine Otter (there is also a twin-engine Otter), was a piston engine commuter aircraft with the excellent capability to operate from very short strips. It was quite a unique machine, with a single, large piston engine and space for 4-5 passengers and a flight crew of two pilots, seated side by side. It was a slow aircraft, but a good work horse. It had a peculiar control stick that could be shifted from left to right and vice versa, depending on which pilot was to fly. To shift it from one side to another, a small locking plunger at the bottom had to be operated and the control stick heaved over to the desired side, ensuring that it got locked there. It also had a steerable tail wheel for ease of manoeuvring in restricted spaces on ground.

We did occasional commuter flights on this aircraft, between Kanpur and Maintenance Command Headquarters at Nagpur. Once, I was detailed to ferry our C-in-C Maintenance Command, Air Marshal OP Mehra, from Kanpur to Nagpur, and to return the same day. It was a hot summer day with poor visibility due to dust haze. We took off at about 11 am and landed at Nagpur at 1.30pm, in hot and bumpy conditions. After seeing off the C-in-C, I got the aircraft refuelled, had a quick bite, and set off for the return journey. I reached Kanpur in the evening, after another long flight in hot and bumpy conditions. To add to my woes, the landing conditions at Kanpur were most unfriendly, with a 17 knots cross-wind gusting up to 25 knots. After landing, the aircraft swung viciously to right due to the strong cross- wind. I applied full left rudder to control it, and even used harsh left brake, but the swing could not be contained and we went off the runway on to the grass shoulder. The only time in my entire flying career when such a thing has happened. I taxied back and switched off, feeling quite sheepish. Neither the flying control nor anyone else had noticed the occurrence due to the poor visibility. However, I confessed to the ground crew, and got the aircraft checked for possible over-stressing of the undercarriage. Fortunately, there was no damage to the aircraft. But I could not say the same for my pride!

VAMPIRE

We had both the single seat as well as the dual seat Vampires. The single seat version was not cleared for spinning. However, the dual seat Vampire had a much wider front fuselage to accommodate the two pilots side by side. This resulted in some change in its aerodynamics, enabling spins to be carried out safely. We would, therefore, carry out spins on it to left and right as part of our test schedule, and check that recovery was satisfactory. Sometimes, we would get a 'rogue' aircraft which, while recovering from a spin to one side, would promptly enter a spin to the opposite side. One had to be on one's toes to neutralize the rudder smartly the moment the spin stopped. A slight delay and you were into another unwanted spin. It was a bit disconcerting, since there was always a nagging possibility of not being able to come out of it, but happily, it never happened.

A spin can occur when an aircraft has 'stalled' on account of high angle of attack (i.e. the angle relative to the flow). This high angle causes a major disturbance to the airflow over the wings, with consequent loss in lift, making the aircraft *stall* and sink. At this point, if for some reason, the aircraft yaws to one side, it would get into a spin. The aircraft nose then drops downwards, and it rolls and yaws and pitches in a random corkscrewing fashion, with rapid loss of altitude. The motion of the aircraft is automatic,(also called 'autorotation'), and the aircraft is at the mercy of the inter-play between aerodynamic and inertial forces, taking the pilot for an unwanted and vigorous ride !! Pilot's controls are not responsive in the normal fashion anymore and only way to recover is to apply and hold certain well-established control inputs, which aim to stop the rotation of the aircraft and reduce the angle of attack. Recovery often takes another turn or two.

As a rule, light trainer aircraft are safe to spin, and recovery is almost always assured – though on some rare occasions, it may fail to recover. On high speed fighter aircraft, however, recovery is not assured at all, and pilots are warned not to enter a spin. In case a pilot does get into a spin, he would most probably have to eject, like I did on the Gnat.

TOOFANI

The other subsonic fighter aircraft overhauled at Kanpur was the French Ouragon – renamed Toofani by us. This was essentially a ground attack machine with an unusually high level of longitudinal stability. This meant that once properly trimmed, the nose would not move up or down easily, making it a steady platform for weapon delivery. However, this had an adverse effect on aircraft manoeuvrability, and required high control forces which detracted from ease of flying.

The Toofani was difficult to turn on ground while taxying. As it did not have a nose wheel steering system, turning on ground required applying brake only on one main wheel – the side you wanted to turn. The distance between the two main wheels was relatively narrow, reducing the leverage the braking wheel could consequently generate. The pilot thus had to use a lot of brake and engine power to make it turn properly on ground; it was somewhat of a struggle. It had two unique wing tip fuel tanks – one on each side, which gave it an elegant look. We were not allowed to land with any fuel in the tip tanks as the additional weight at the wing tip could cause extra strain on the wing if the landing was hard. However, if for some reason the pilot was forced to land back before the fuel in the tip tanks got consumed, he would have to land with fuel still remaining in the tip tanks. To avoid such an eventuality, a provision was made to jettison the fuel from the tip tanks. It was a pretty sight to see the fuel streaming out from both wing tips, and added a touch of glamour to the Toofani.

MYSTERE

We also had the Mystere coming for flight tests regularly, and I used to have a good time with it; keeping alive my fond memories of Kalaikunda! As I have already covered it earlier, I won`t say anything more about this solid fighter.

HUNTER

We also had the single seat Hunter 56 aircraft, which would come on the flight line almost every day. It was a most beautiful looking fighter and looked really elegant in its camouflage paint. What is more, its flight controls were the most delightful, and its control feel was out of the world!

The term 'control feel' implies the ease with which the pilot's control input produces the precise response that he would wish from the aircraft. It makes for swift and accurate manoeuvring, and thus enhances the overall efficiency of the pilot-machine interface. During the development stage of an aircraft, the test pilot spends a lot of time and effort, along with the designers, to fine-tune the 'control feel' of the aircraft. The Hunter's flight controls provided a magical feel, and I enjoyed carrying out vigorous aerobatics, often at a low altitude over the airfield, much to the delight of the ground crew. On occasion, I would do a really low pass over the runway before pulling up and carrying out a tight curved approach for landing. All very thrilling stuff. However, not everyone thought so!

Once, a visiting ferry pilot witnessed my aerobatics and low run, and on return to his base in Assam, he mentioned it to his colleagues at the bar. To my misfortune, a senior officer from Air Headquarters Flight Safety Directorate, also happened to be at the bar, and overheard the excited narrative. The upshot was a stern letter to my Station Commander from Air Headquarters stating that an aircraft was reported to have carried out 'low level aerobatics followed by a low run at just four feet over the runway. This was in total contravention to IAF rules on flying discipline and safety...' and a copy of the letter was also sent to C-in-C Maintenance Command, Air Marshal Pandit. Sure enough, the C-in-C came over to Kanpur to check on the matter. I was duly summoned to the Station Commander's office to face the C-in-C who naturally gave me the works. Fortunately, he did not wish to take any action which could affect my career. However, a stern warning came through, and I had to express deep regret for my actions. I was sorry to upset my C-in-C as I respected him greatly. But somehow, the joy of making a fighter aircraft do what it was capable of, and that too with a level of expertise and finesse, prevented me from being over-burdened with guilt.

At a later date, the IAF procured a few squadrons of a more powerful version of the Hunter, called Hunter 56 A. This aircraft had provision for carrying extra fuel in two huge 230 gallon drop tanks under the wing roots, in addition to the two standard 100 gallon drop tanks under outer part of the wing. This gave it additional range, and the more powerful engine compensated for the additional weight so that it's performance remained more or less the same as the original Hunter 56. One of these aircraft was once fitted with a new Navigation-and-Attack system called Decca Doppler, and came up for trials in which I participated. I remember doing one sortie where I had to fly low level from Kanpur to Jabalpur and 'attack' a bridge there using the system. It was great not to have to do any map-reading, as the system did it perfectly. I only had to follow an arrow on the instrument to keep me on track, and other data like distance and time to target was displayed on the panel. I could whizz past at tree-top height and just wait for the target to appear at the stipulated time. And it did, with great precision. I pulled up and carried out a mock attack and returned to base, again at low level, and landed back – the entire flight being guided with utmost precision. Most modern fighters now have inertial navigation and attack systems, which are even better, greatly reducing pilot workload and anxiety.

On another day, I undertook a similar flight on the Hunter at low level to mock-attack a railway bridge at a place called Sawai Madhopur, in Rajasthan. Everything went as planned, and I reached the target bridge dead on time. I carried out a mock bomb attack on the bridge, and as a matter of standard procedure, pressed the bomb button. Immediately, there was a big bang, and when I looked over the wings, I found that both my 230-gallon drop tanks had been jettisoned. They were huge tanks, and still had a lot of fuel in them, which I had now lost. I had to climb up to get to economical cruise conditions to return to base. After landing, when the ground technicians checked the electrical circuits of the weapon system, they found a short circuit which had caused the tanks to jettison. Later, we were relieved to hear that the tanks had fallen in a safe area, and did not do any damage.

ILYUSHIN-14

On one occasion, an Ilyushin-14 transport aircraft of the IAF had landed at Kanpur with some engine trouble. This was a 30-35 seater aircraft of Russian design, with two piston engines. Apparently, one of the engines had a burst cylinder, and the whole engine had to be replaced. The job was taken up by No.1 BRD and completed in two weeks time. The aircraft was then ready for flight with the new engine. But no pilot at the station had any experience on this type of aircraft. However, the station commander wanted to know if any of the test pilots there could check out the new engine in the air before the ferry crew were called. I jumped at the thought of flying a transport aircraft on which I had no experience, and readily agreed to do the needful. I required some publications on the aircraft to learn about its systems and handling characteristics and so on before leaping into the air. But, unfortunately, no such publications were available at Kanpur.

Early Years as a Test Pilot

This put me in a bit of a fix, when someone told me that there was a technical officer on station who had been with an Ilyushin-14 Squadron of the IAF some years back. When I got in touch with this officer, he said he had been an engineer on this aircraft at one time. Fortunately, he managed to dig out some hand written notes with information about its systems, but nothing regarding its flying qualities, limitations and emergency procedures. Anyway, I spent some time with the engineer in the cockpit and familiarized myself with its various systems, controls, switches and so on. I had to use my knowledge of aircraft in general, and a bit of imagination, to figure out the emergency drills as best as possible. I carried out a few engine ground runs, and learnt the procedures for engine switch off and restart in the air. Once I got familiar with the engine operation, I felt more comfortable to carry out a test flight.

The next morning, I got into the aircraft with the engineer in the co-pilot's seat. We started the engines and carried out the standard ground checks, checking all engine parameters up to full power. All was well and within the stipulated limit; the propellers ran smoothly with a healthy, regular beat. I taxied out slowly, checking the foot brakes, which were excellent. The aircraft did not have a nose wheel steer and I had to use differential braking to turn, as in the Vampire and Toofani. But it was quite easy to manage.

We lined up on the runway, and opened full power, holding on to the brakes. A quick check of the engine parameters revealed that all was OK. I released brakes and the aircraft accelerated fairly well. The rudder was quite effective to keep the aircraft on the centre line. As the speed built up, I got the stick back gently to lift the nose wheel just a little off the runway, and held it there. As I had no idea about the take-off speed, I let it get airborne on its own to ensure that I did not get her off prematurely. We got airborne quite comfortably at a little higher speed, and put her into a gentle climb. I throttled the engines to climb power, maintaining a speed which gave a reasonable rate of climb. As we reached an altitude of 8,000ft, I levelled off and reduced power to cruise setting. I maintained level flight for 10 to 15 minutes, carrying out some turns and manipulating the engine controls, also just looking around to get familiar with the cockpit environment and the feel of the controls. The response of the controls and general behaviour of the aircraft and engine were pretty classic, and soon I felt perfectly comfortable.

It was then time to check its stalling speed. As it was a proven aircraft, I did not expect any problem with the stall. However, since I had no information about the stall speed, I had to approach it with caution. So, I throttled back the engines to idle power, and held the nose up to reduce speed gently, being careful to check the control response. There was no noticeable aerodynamic buffet to warn the imminence of stall, but the stall itself was gentle enough with a clear nose drop, and a comfortable recovery. I repeated the stall once more with landing flaps lowered, and found it quite satisfactory.

Thereafter, I switched off one engine and flew for a while on a single engine and found the aircraft behaviour quite typical. I restarted the engine and repeated the same procedure with the other engine with no problem. Since I had now established the stall speed, I could work out the best speeds for approach and landing. I made a longish approach and managed quite a smooth landing. There was no problem keeping her on the centre line and coming to stop. I carried out a few more take-offs and landings to get more confidence in the machine, before calling it a day. The next day I took up a few other Test Pilots on the station to let them get a feel of the aircraft.

I was really elated that I had managed the test flight safely, with no prior knowledge of the aircraft. After all, that is what Test Pilots are expected to do.

Aircraft and Armament Testing Unit

AIR FORCE KANPUR

HF 24, Marut

In February 1966, I got posted to Aircraft and Armament Testing Unit (A&ATU) at Kanpur. The new indigenous fighter aircraft HF24, was in the process of being certified for the IAF. Three of the pre-production aircraft had been allotted to A&ATU for service evaluation trials, as a prelude to eventual induction into the IAF. I had been eagerly waiting to lay my hands on this new fighter ever since I returned from Test Pilot's course in UK, and now I had my chance.

The HF24 was designed to be a two engine supersonic fighter with Mach 2.0 capability. The chief designer of the aircraft was Mr. Kurt Tank, a celebrated German designer of Messerschmitt fame, who was deputed to HAL Bangalore where the aircraft was designed in collaboration with Indian designers. By the time I joined A&ATU in 1966, a number of prototypes had been put through the development stages at HAL Bangalore and now we had to evaluate the aircraft for the IAF.

As the aircraft was designed for supersonic flight with radar interception capability, its airframe had all the attributes of a supersonic fighter. However, a Russian engine that was to have been developed for it did not materialize for various reasons. A few other engines were evaluated for integration into the airframe, but were not found suitable. Left high and dry, the designers finally fitted two British Orpheus engines on it. This small engine powered the Folland Gnat aircraft, still in production at HAL Bangalore. The engine too was being produced there. However, the Orpheus engine produced only 4,520 pounds of thrust, the two engines together thus giving the aircraft a little over 9,000 pounds of thrust. This was way below the requirement for supersonic performance. The aircraft was therefore, sadly relegated to the transonic category, and we at A&ATU were to evaluate it as a transonic ground attack fighter. It was still a promising machine in that role, and we took to it with enthusiasm, eager to put it through its paces and to explore all it could do.

When I joined A&ATU, its Commanding Officer was Wg.Cdr. 'Scorpy' Ghosh, an old time Test Pilot, known for his superior technical knowledge. He would often gather us in the crew room, take to the blackboard and write some long-winding formulae on it and then question us on what it meant. More often than not, we would have no clue. He would then tutor us on the theories involved. However, he never interfered with the flying programme and we went ahead with vigour to explore the aircraft's capabilities without any reservation. We were a tight bunch of test pilots: Sqn. Ldr. Karan Yadav, who was earlier my boss at ATFF, Sqn. Ldr. P.Singh, Sqn. Ldr. Brijesh Jayal (Jay), Sqn. Ldr. Sapre and myself.

The HF-24 (later named Marut), was a long, sleek aircraft with swept wings, and had the two Orpheus 703 jet engines imbedded side by side in its rear fuselage. The pilot's cockpit was pretty high up, requiring a tall ladder to access it. It had a long sliding canopy, which was electrically operated. Its hydraulically operated flight controls had provision for manual operation, should the hydraulic system fail. It had foot pedal operated wheel brakes, and a nose wheel steering system operated by rudder pedal movement – the first fighter in the IAF to have nose wheel steering, and a big novelty for us.

Its weaponry consisted of four 30mm Aden guns embedded in the front fuselage - two on each side, and two pylon stations under each wing, to carry 100-gallon fuel drop tanks or bombs or rockets in any combination. In addition, it had a provision for carrying 55 high-speed rockets of 68mm calibre in the fuselage right under the cockpit, just like in Mystere. Altogether, the fire power of HF-24 was formidable, and it proved its mettle in the 1971 Indo- Pak war against enemy tanks in the Rajasthan sector.

The 'g' limit recommended for the aircraft in the draft Pilot's Manual was just 5.5 g, a rather low limit for a high-speed fighter aircraft. This implied poor turning rate at high speeds, something unacceptable in terms of combat capability. I was intrigued that against a design clearance of 7.0 g, the HF 24 could only muster 5.5 g. I got down to a detailed study of various aerodynamic factors which could cause such a shortfall, and compared the HF 24 with other fighters which were cleared to 7.0 g and beyond. After such a comparison, I came to the conclusion that the HF24 had the capability to attain 7.0 g, and that 5.5 g was an unrealistic limit imposed on it. With such a limit, it was difficult to carry out full aerobatic manoeuvres comfortably, and indeed, nobody seemed to have pushed it to that end. I felt that for a fighter aircraft not to be easily aerobatic, was a scandalous situation, and was desperately keen to explore this aspect, and to push it to its flight limit of 7.0g.

After I had done my first solo on the aircraft, I immediately started to explore its 'g' envelope, to see if it could reach 7g. I found that the aircraft buffeted rather easily in turns, and as the turn was tightened towards higher g, the buffet increased substantially. Buffeting is a phenomenon which occurs when the airflow over the wings is disturbed (or broken) due to high angle of attack. This disturbed air flow also hits the tail plane at the rear end and shakes up the whole aircraft. It is somewhat like driving a car on a rough road. It is a bit uncomfortable, but as long as control of the aircraft is not affected, it is not a big deal. However, it does create a lot of drag, causing the speed to wash off rather rapidly, not a desirable feature.

I carried out progressively tighter turns to increase the 'g' beyond 5.5 g and found that nothing much happened other than an increase in the buffet level. There was no controllability problem right up to 7g. This gave me the confidence to carry out aerobatic manoeuvres. I had, of course, to put up with the high rate of speed decay. After a little practice away from the airfield, I came overhead and carried out full aerobatics at a low level to show off the aircraft's capability.

When I landed back and switched off the aircraft near the hangar, the ground crew placed the ladder to the cockpit as per standard practice. As I descended, I found the crew lined up on either side, waiting with a garland and sweets! They were overjoyed to see 'their' aircraft showing its capabilities – something they had not seen before. I was gratified at getting such a response. What intrigued me, however, was how they had managed to get a garland and sweets so quickly! It showed how sensitive they were to 'their' aircraft's performance. I was happy that I had broken the ice, and proved the 5.5 g limit to be a bogey.

We carried out fairly intensive flight testing of the HF 24 during the years 1966 to 67. As already mentioned, my very first observation was the excessive buffet that was experienced in turns. Along with it, the longitudinal stability was found to be poor. This resulted in poor control feel of the aircraft in the pitching plane (i.e. for nose up and down). Accurate pitch control at low speeds, such as during approach and landing was, therefore, somewhat difficult.

We were given the threshold speed for landing as 155 knots, i.e. the speed to be kept when crossing the beginning of the runway. At this speed, the aircraft was already in buffet and pitch control being poor, made it difficult to manage a smooth landing. And when the aircraft touched down with a bit of a thump, the nose wheel would promptly drop down on to the runway due to inertia effect, and could not be pulled up again. This was because on the HF24, the main wheels were located rather far back under the fuselage, thus reducing the leverage the elevators at the tail could generate on ground. So, once the nose wheel came down on to the runway surface, it was not possible to rotate the aircraft back into a nose-up attitude that it had at touchdown. Now, when you get into such a 3- point attitude just after touchdown, the aerodynamic drag on the aircraft is minimal, as there is relatively small frontal area against the wind to create a significant rearward drag force. So, the aircraft hurtles down at high speed, eating up a lot of runway. Consequently, the wheel brakes have to be applied at a higher speed to stop within the available runway length. This causes the brakes to get heated up excessively and the tyres to get worn out faster. All this because the aircraft's nose could not be held up after touch down to provide aerodynamic braking to decelerate it to some lower speed before brakes are applied. To me, it was obvious that it was necessary to get a reasonably smooth landing in order to ensure that the nose does not thump down and could then be held up to provide aerodynamic braking. The only way to do this was to have better longitudinal control at landing, which was possible if we had a higher speed at the threshold.

So, on my next flight, I increased the threshold speed from 155 knots to 170 knots, a rather bold jump. I found that it was then possible, and even easy, to get a smooth landing, and to hold the nose up till the speed reduced to around 125 knots when the nose would drop down. Thereafter, moderate braking was enough to come to a halt. The brakes as well as tyres were much cooler, and the landing distance was much *shorter* than when we came to land at the lower speed of 155 knots. From that time onwards, we came into land with 170 knots at the threshold, and found it altogether much more comfortable.

The recommended speed for takeoff was also 155 knots. This was more or less the lowest speed at which one could get airborne. At this speed the angle of attack of the aircraft was relatively high, resulting in extra aerodynamic drag, which in turn made acceleration after getting airborne rather poor. This became strikingly evident when my friend Jay, one day, got airborne at Jamnagar with a heavy bomb load and found the aircraft would neither accelerate nor climb. As he was too close to the runway surface he did not dare to retract the undercarriage, which added to the drag. I was at the control tower watching the takeoff. The aircraft continued at a height of just a few feet above ground right till the end of the runway, beyond which it kicked up a lot of dust. We thought we were about to witness a crash, but as luck would have it, the ground there was sloping down a bit and Jay just made it. After this experience we immediately increased our takeoff speed also to 170 knots, which gave us reasonable acceleration after getting airborne and avoided the uncalled-for brinkmanship. Of course the takeoff length increased as a result, but we had to accept that in the interest of safety.

The designers had apparently anticipated poor elevator effectiveness at takeoff and had made a unique provision to tackle the problem. A lever was provided in the cockpit, which when operated, extended the nose undercarriage oleo leg hydraulically, thus raising the nose mechanically to make up for poor elevator effectiveness. However, with an increase in takeoff speed to 170 knots such tricks were not required, and the device was de-activated.

We had taken one HF24 to Halwara (Ludhiana) in the summer of 1967 to carry out hot weather trials. As part of these trials, I was assigned to establish a safe get-away speed if one engine failed soon after getting airborne. I had to takeoff with full load (4 full fuel drop tanks) at the peak day temperature of 48 degrees C. Here too, I found that the lowest safe speed was 170 knots, when even with one engine failed, the aircraft could still gradually accelerate and pull away. Thus 170 knots became the speed to swear by.

Even though the aircraft was underpowered, its clean lines ensured that with both engines at full throttle, it could still clock 600 knots at low altitudes. This was a terrific speed to have for getting away safely after attacking the target. During the 1971 Indo-Pak war, our pilots exploited this feature to great effect after dropping their bombs or firing their rockets at the targets. The aircraft not being suited for a dog fight, the sensible thing was to run away to safety after the attack. At 600 knots at tree-top level, no one could catch the home-bound HF24 !

One could well ask the question- how an under-powered HF24 could attain a top speed of 600 knots in level flight. There are two reasons for this. Firstly, its clean aerodynamic shape minimises the drag increase with increase in speed. The other factor is the design of its long engine air intakes. This causes greater build up of air pressure in the intake with increase in speed, resulting in higher air mass flow through the engine, giving higher thrust as the speed increases. On the HF 24, thus, the drag increase at higher speeds is minimized, and the thrust increase is maximized. The net result is good acceleration and higher max speed. Of course, it would stop accelerating at a speed where the thrust and drag equalise. On the HF24, at low altitudes this happens at around 600 knots, which is quite commendable, and a clear plus point for the aircraft.

The equation at low speeds is, sort of reversed. As the air mass flow through the engine is less at lower speeds, the thrust reduces. Also, now the major contributor to drag is not skin friction or body shape, since the speed is low, but the large angle of attack required at low speeds. This (induced) drag is quite high, and more so in a turn, on account of the excessive buffet. Thus, in a tight turn at low speeds, the HF 24 decelerates rapidly even at full throttle. This is the reason for the aircraft not being suitable for dog fights. In fact, this phenomenon is applicable to all jet fighters, but what makes it rather critical for the HF 24 is its low thrust to start with, which makes it decelerate much faster than other aircraft. And whichever aircraft loses speed faster in a dog fight loses the fight!

Another peculiar result of the combination of low aerodynamic drag increase at high speeds, and a relatively high rise in thrust, is that the rate of climb is not sensitive to climbing speeds. On most aircraft, there is one optimum speed at which you get the best rate of climb, but this did not strictly apply to the HF 24. We tried climbs at different speeds, ranging from 350 knots (0.75 Mach) to 550 knots (0.9 Mach), and found to our surprise, that the time taken to climb to 30,000 ft remained virtually constant! The thrust increase with increase in speed apparently "balanced out" the increase in drag, making the HF 24 unique in this respect!

Yet another benefit of excellent intake performance was improved stability of the engine in 'slam' acceleration. This involves slamming the throttles from idle power to full power in about one second, and checking the engine stability and the time taken to reach max RPM, which has to be within given limits. This is an operational requirement on fighter aircraft. On the HF 24, we found that we met the stipulated acceleration time without any difficulty, and the engine accelerated to max power quite smoothly. The same engine on the Gnat would, often give engine surge and flame out during this test. And it would need much fine tuning to avoid the surge. I think it was the long air intakes on the HF 24 which gave it the benefit of greater engine stability – the intake on the Gnat was very short as it was a much smaller aircraft.

For one reason or another, we had to carry out frequent ferries between Kanpur and HAL Bangalore and vice versa, with a refuelling stop at Nagpur. We would cruise at 30,000 ft at 0.9 Mach. At such heights, the longitudinal stability of an aircraft normally deteriorates a bit due to lower air density. But, on the HF 24, we found it to be much worse than expected. If during cruise, we let-go of the control stick even for a few seconds, the aircraft would start pitching up, and if left to its devices, it would even stall. We had to be on our toes all the time to prevent such outrageous behaviour! Normally, if the nose goes up due to (say) turbulence, the natural stability of the aircraft would tend to bring it down to its original position. But on the HF24, the stability margins were so narrow that at higher altitudes, it would actually become unstable, and just continue to depart from its original position. On later models, the wing chord (i.e. the width of the wing) was increased significantly to improve its stability characteristics. It also resulted in marked reduction in buffet. But in the early models, we had to accept some unwanted rock 'n roll.

The supersonic aerodynamic design of the aircraft with its mass concentrated along the fuselage naturally made it prone to the phenomenon of *inertia coupling*. However, its behaviour was totally different from that of other high speed fighter aircraft. While the average high speed fighter would get into a roll-YAW coupling, the HF24 would get into a roll-PITCH coupling, a virtually unknown term hitherto. This was due to its longitudinal stability being worse than it's directional stability, and the divergence would always occur towards the weaker side. In a sustained rapid roll on the HF 24, one could feel the 'g' building up as the roll progresses, and the pilot needed to keep on pushing the sick forward to prevent it. On the MiG 21, like most high speed aircraft, one has to keep on squeezing the rudder to avoid excessive sideslip building up, as there the directional stability is worse than longitudinal stability. The HF 24, thus, has the distinction of having a new term (roll PITCH coupling), coined in its honour!

We carried out air to ground weapons trials at Jamnagar during November 1966 and May 1967. This involved two-gun firing, rocket firing and bombing. We got good scores in all these modes and the aircraft proved to be a steady weapons platform. In one bombing sortie, I made two dives, dropping one 1,000 pound bomb in each dive, and both bombs scored a direct hit on the pin. A bit of luck, of course, but thrilling all the same.

While I was in A&ATU, the aircraft was cleared only for two gun firing. So, we never got to fire all four guns simultaneously. However, after I had left A&ATU on deputation to HAL Kanpur, the task of testing all four guns firing simultaneously was allotted to A& ATU. By then, HAL test pilots at Bangalore had carried out a large number of gunnery flights, but could not clear the aircraft for four gun firing, as they had encountered severe vibrations during firing.

Normally, A&ATU would undertake such trials only after initial clearance by HAL test pilots. However, this procedure was dispensed with in view of the imminence of the 1971 Indo-Pak war. Thus, to save time, the responsibility to clear all four guns to fire simultaneously was handed over directly to A&ATU, and Sqn. Ldr. A.K. Sapre was allotted the task. He flew the aircraft down to Jamnagar and carried out the firing on the range located by the sea side there. He too experienced severe vibrations when all four guns were fired. Due to the vibrations, some electrical circuits tripped and reverted the flying controls to manual mode. This caused a serious controllability problem, but he managed to regain control and landed back safely, quite shaken up. The technical staff carried out some adjustments and offered the aircraft for flight the next day. The pilot again experienced severe vibrations, and again the controls reverted to manual. However, this time he was not able to regain control of the aircraft and had to eject.

His parachute deployed all right, but he was over the sea, and landed in water. Unfortunately, his body was never found. It was a truly sad story and we lost a fine test pilot and an exceptional human being. It is a million dollar question as to why such a test had to be undertaken when all evidence available indicated near-certain recurrence of a serious control problem.

In August 1967, I was detailed to carry out Radar Interception trials on two HF 24 aircraft, which were fitted with the AIRPASS (Airborne Interception Radar Pilot Attack Sighting System). This was the latest British Interception Radar fitted on their 'Lightning' supersonic interceptor. It was the most advanced Airborne interception radar system at that time, and I was flattered to have been given the task. Air Commodore Moolgavkar (later Air Chief Marshal and Chief of Air Staff), who was Director, Policy and Plans Directorate at Air Headquarters, personally rang me up about selecting me for the trials, and said I could directly contact him should I face any problems during the trials.

A British engineer from Ferranti company was deputed to India to oversee the integration of the radar on HF24, and to provide necessary support for the trials. He had numerous sessions with me on the intricacies of the radar and its operation, and briefed me in detail on the various modes to be tested. The then existing fighter aircraft of IAF (Mystere, Hunter and Gnat) also had a small radar installed in the nose, but this was only capable of giving the pilot the distance of the target and nothing more. The pilot had to first acquire the target visually and then point the aircraft towards it and only then would the range information be available. Naturally, this was of no use at night or in bad weather when the pilot could not make visual contact with the target.

The AIRPASS had the capability to pick up the target a good 50km away and guide the pilot both in direction and height towards it with great accuracy. It could also give a command to the pilot to fire the missile at the appropriate range, without even sighting the target visually. It was thus, fully effective in bad weather or at night. The system provided a quantum jump in airborne interception capability and there was an air of excitement in the trials. The trials were held at HAL Bangalore during August/September 1967. One IAF Canberra bomber aircraft with crew was positioned at Bangalore to act as a target. I carried out some 15 odd flights, attacking the target from various angles and heights. These were recorded on board, and later analyzed by the engineers. I must have carried out at least 25 attacks during the trials, each one being pursued till the 'FIRE' and 'BREAK OFF' commands came up on the screen. On a few occasions, I was inside cloud, and completed the attack without making visual contact. Altogether, the system proved to be excellent, and I gave it big thumbs up. Soon after that, I was detailed to carry out similar interception trials on the MiG 21 aircraft, for purposes of comparison. I landed up at Chandigarh, where the first MiG 21 squadrons were located, and flew a number of flights evaluating its interception radar, thoroughly enjoying flying the first Mach 2.0 fighter of the IAF. The radar performance of the MiG 21 was also very good, though the range was not as good as that of AIRPASS. However, a number of innovative features made it easier to operate and made it more pilot friendly.

xxxxxx

The airspace over and around Chakeri airfield at Kanpur was often full of birds, spiralling up in large numbers, particularly during summer months. This was a major hazard to flying aircraft. There would also be a lot of dust haze which would reduce the visibility, making detection of birds in the air even more difficult. I often found myself in the thick of this circus with birds whizzing past too close for comfort. I realized that taking evasive action at the last moment was not the answer. When you do an abrupt turn to avoid a bird, you cannot judge your flight path accurately as the aircraft is not going where the nose is pointing, because of the high angle of attack. Further, in a tight turn, you present a larger wing area to an on-coming bird, thus increasing the chances of a hit. I found that maintaining near level flight, with small corrections to one's heading, was a far safer course. There was invariably much more space between birds than what appears from a distance, and a sleek aircraft like a fighter, can easily slip through between birds without coming to harm, as long as the pilot aims accurately at the gaps. I followed such a practice and never hit a bird.

During the Indo-Pak war of 1965, the Test Pilots at Kanpur were allotted the additional task of ferrying fighters like Hunters and Mysteres to forward bases to replace the losses, and we did numerous such ferries. IAF station Kanpur had huge hangars where fighter aircraft in large numbers were stored, but we had no anti-aircraft batteries there to protect the same. I thought it would be a juicy target for Pakistan to carry out an attack from their Eastern wing (i.e. East Pakistan). I calculated that it was just possible for them to undertake a bombing mission at dusk from there, and return in the fading light. It would, of course be marginal on fuel, but I felt a daring pilot could do it. I suggested that we put up a Combat Air Patrol (CAP) in the evening, with a Gnat aircraft armed with loaded guns. The Station Commander was hesitant, but I emphasized that an attack by the enemy could cause unacceptable damage to scores of fighter aircraft kept in storage there. He finally agreed and I began patrolling the airfield in a Gnat every evening, hoping that a Pakistani Canberra would show up. It would have been an easy target for the Gnat. However, it did not happen, but we were at least prepared for such an eventuality.

Those days, we had regular drill parades on Monday mornings, where almost the whole station would participate. Many officers merely tolerated this age-old ritual of military life, but I really looked forward to it. One had to make sure that the uniform was well starched and neat, all brass items on it polished and shining bright. The shoes too had to be polished to a mirror-like shine. There had to be a close haircut so that strands of hair did not peep out from under the cap. While doing the drill manoeuvres, one had to stamp the foot hard on the tarmac with a sharp sound, the movement being crisp and robot-like. I used to have a special pair of black shoes with a hard sole, so that I could create a resounding thump when I stamped it hard on the tarmac. All these and the loud and clear words of command that one had to shout, somehow made the whole process very exciting to me. In fact, it was a meticulous show of discipline, determination and pride in service – all symbolic, but very effective and inspiring. And I loved it.

xxxxxx

During my stay in A&ATU, Jay and I had become very good friends. We were both highly motivated to put the HF24 through its paces. I still remember how during winter months, between flights, we would often pace up and down the small road in front of the Flight Office, enjoying the sun and discussing various aspects of the HF 24, and our experiences of the previous flight. Jay was an exceptional officer, with impeccable integrity and a forthright personality. I greatly valued his friendship – it added freshness and good cheer to my working days at A&ATU.

Later, when I had gone on deputation to HAL Kanpur on the Avro, Jay was on deputation to HAL Nasik as a Test Pilot on the MiG 21 aircraft. Whenever I flew the Avro over from Kanpur to Santa Cruz airport at Bombay to carryout Instrument Landing Approaches at night, I would stop over at Ojhar, Nasik and spend some time with Jay and fly the MiG 21 when possible. In due course, Jay returned to the Airforce mainstream and rose to the rank of Air Marshal, first taking over as Deputy Chief of Air Staff, and later, had two tenures as Commander-in-Chief, first at Eastern Air Command, and then at South-West Air Command, winding up a brilliant career with flying colours.

xxxxxx

In April 1967, we were blessed with our second child, a son, at Air force hospital Kanpur. I remember waiting anxiously outside the delivery room for the event. Soon after his arrival, the nurse brought him out, all wrapped up, for me to have a quick glimpse. When I saw him from close, I was quite amazed that he had wide open eyes, which he slanted in my direction as if to size me up! It is my good luck that he did not persist with such behaviour when he grew up!

Test Flying Transport Aircraft and Gliders

Hindustan Aeronautics Ltd Kanpur

HS 748 Avro, Rohini & Ardhra

It was in August 1968, when I was in the thick of test flying activity on the HF-24 fighter aircraft at A&ATU, that I got orders to move to HAL Kanpur on deputation, where the 44 seater turboprop aircraft, HS- 748 (AVRO) was being manufactured under license. I had hoped that I would be deputed to HAL Bangalore where I could have continued with HF-24 flight testing, a task in which I had been deeply involved. But Air Headquarters thought that I was better utilized in flight testing of transport aircraft. I was surprised and disappointed at this decision of Air HQ. But Providence has its own reasons for pushing you into unexpected spots – and not only to punish you! It turned out to be a blessing in disguise. Not only did I learn a lot about transport aircraft, but more importantly, got a unique opportunity to explore the amazing limits to which you could push a transport aircraft. It was the most gratifying experience for me as a test pilot, and I would forever cherish it.

I requested Air HQ to give me clearance to continue to fly aircraft at A&ATU as well as at No.1 Base Repair Depot (BRD), both located at Kanpur. Fortunately for me, my request was processed by some of my well-wishers at Air HQ, and in no time at all, I had a letter in my hand authorizing me to fly all military aircraft at IAF Station Kanpur, as and when required. Both A&ATU and No.1 BRD were only too happy to have the services of one more Test Pilot at their disposal. This enabled me to keep in touch with fighter aircraft on a regular basis, and I simply loved it. I was able to lay my hands on Hunters, Mysteres, Toofanis, Vampires, MiG21s and Sukhoi-7, while flogging the Avro full time.

At HAL Kanpur I was the only Test Pilot for a long time and had to manage without a co-pilot. It was a challenging situation and I had to put in some hard work to manage. I burnt the midnight oil studying the flight manuals thoroughly and at the same time took cautious steps in the air to explore the aircraft's characteristics. Initially, I 'borrowed' a co-pilot from among other pilots on the station, none of whom had any experience on the AVRO. They were nevertheless, of help in the air. Later, when I could not get any other pilot to act as co-pilot, I would take a senior technician in the right hand seat to carry out some simple co-pilot tasks pertaining to aircraft systems. This arrangement carried on for some years, when finally in 1973, a pilot was inducted to act as my co-pilot.

The HS 748 was nicknamed Avro, after the name of the British company which designed it. Both the IAF and Indian Airlines had placed large orders for the aircraft. HAL Kanpur had its hands full with the manufacture of the aircraft and consequently, there was abundance of test flying activity, much to my delight. The aircraft was pretty conventional in design, with manual flight controls, a good Auto Pilot and communication systems as well as weather radar. The only relatively complex item was its two turbo-prop engines. A turbo-prop (short for turbine-propeller), is basically a jet engine driving a propeller to create forward thrust. Such an arrangement is more complicated than a pure jet engine, but has the advantage of good fuel economy. Hence it was a popular option for airlines. Of course, the propeller would restrict the aircraft speed to a degree. But, compared to piston engine aircraft, it had higher power and speed and was in a way, a stepping stone to the jet airliners of today.

The production flight test schedule of the HS748 called for tests to be done at 'high weight, forward C.G. (centre of gravity)' as one configuration, and 'low weight, aft C.G'. as another configuration. Big boxes of ballast weights would be placed towards the front of the fuselage or at rear to get the requisite C.G. The high weight configuration was required for all single engine climb tests. The aircraft had to attain a minimum gradient of climb of 2.4 per cent with the right engine switched off and the left engine at full power. This was a certification requirement and had to be met before the aircraft could be passed on to the customer.

We would often find engines not meeting this crucial requirement and it would entail replacement with a new engine. The single engine climb tests would then need to be repeated. It was a rather wasteful effort, but we had to put up with it. The low weight tests included climb to the maximum cruising altitude of 25,000 ft and numerous handling quality checks, including single engine controllability. And of course, all the aircraft systems needed to be tested as per laid down schedules. One important test was to check the Instrument Landing System (ILS) of the aircraft. Since Kanpur airfield did not have the required ground installation, we had to fly to other airfields equipped with this facility, to check the ILS. We would often go to Agra for the test and would carry out a non-stop flight for the purpose. Sometimes this test would be done at Delhi, and we would carry ground crew in the aircraft to prepare it for flight the next day, and have a small get together in the evening.

The Indian Airlines Case

In December 1970, Indian Airlines pilots of HS-748 Avro aircraft based in Bombay went on strike to protest against poor performance of the aircraft. I was sent from HAL Kanpur to look into the problem. I arrived in Bombay and the same evening, a bunch of Indian Airlines' pilots came to my hotel room, ostensibly to apprise me of their complaints about the performance of the aircraft. Their ulterior motive, however, seemed to be to influence me to support their cause regarding the strike, and duly took out a bottle of scotch to help the process! I accepted one drink as a matter of courtesy, while assuring them that I would not hesitate in telling the truth about the aircraft performance, and that as a Test Pilot, I was honour bound to do so. They were duly mollified.

The next day, I carried out test flights on a few of the aircraft. I found that the climb and cruise performance of the aircraft was indeed well below the figures stipulated in the Flight Manual. When I mentioned this after landing, the pilots were jubilant, as it justified their stand to proceed on strike. In the turbo-prop engine fitted on the Avro, you set the stipulated RPM for the cruise, and then fine-tune the fuel flow by using a fuel-trimmer switch to get the exact recommended turbine temperature. I found that not only was the cruise speed attained much lower than stipulated, but even the fuel flow was much lower than expected. This indicated that there was insufficient air-flow through the engine compressor, causing the stipulated temperature to be reached at a lower fuel flow, resulting in lower thrust. When I asked the engineers if the compressor efficiency could be improved, which would increase the air flow, they answered in the affirmative. The next day, they carried out what is called a compressor 'wash', to clean the compressor blades of any deposits or corrosion, which could degrade their efficiency. After this was done, I flew the aircraft and found that there was a clear improvement in the performance. Some additional work was also carried out to reduce the aerodynamic drag of the aircraft. When these rectifications were completed on the fleet, I flight tested all the aircraft and found that they all met the required performance. When I suggested to the Indian Airline pilots that they could fly the aircraft and see for themselves that the performance was now up to the mark, they declined to do so.

It transpired that one of their Operations managers had been suspended as he had joined the strike in spite of the fact that the management level pilots were not permitted to participate in such strikes. The Indian Commercial Pilots Association (ICPA), which had engineered the strike, wanted to prove that the aircraft was unsafe to operate, so that the operations manager would be deemed to have joined the strike in the interest of public safety. If that was proved, his suspension could be revoked. Thus, even though their legitimate complaint of poor performance had been fully resolved, they now raised a bogie that they did not have confidence in the single engine take-off performance of the aircraft. They requested me to demonstrate to them a single engine take off at maximum weight. Now, such a test is to be conducted under carefully controlled conditions, and is normally done only at the early certification testing stage. Even the production flight test schedule does not call for such a test. This is so because the test itself involves too high a risk and is not worth repeating after the certification stage. What is required in the flight test schedule, however, is to carry out single engine climbs at maximum weight at a safe height, and to ensure that the stipulated minimum rate of climb is attainable. This indirectly ensures that the minimum takeoff climb gradient would be achieved in the event of an engine failure on take-off. The possibility of such an occurrence itself is so rare, that it is considered acceptable if the aircraft can climb at a relatively poor gradient, as long as it can clear obstacles on the take-off path with a certain minimum margin. The margins are however, narrow, and hence the implicit risk.

I was not comfortable carrying out a single engine take-off on the aircraft, as I had never done so earlier. As I said, the production flight test schedule did not call for it. But there was tremendous psychological pressure on me, since my refusing to do so would imply that even I, as the Test Pilot, did not have confidence in the aircraft's performance. How then, could the airline pilots be expected to have confidence? What is more, they carry fare-paying passengers and their safety was also in question.

Under the circumstances, I felt duty bound to demonstrate that the aircraft would climb away safely even after losing an engine on the take-off run. So, I agreed to demonstrate such a take-off - who else would? I had confidence in the aircraft's capability since I had myself flight tested and cleared all their Avro aircraft after manufacture at HAL Kanpur, and had made sure that their single-engine climb performance was up to the mark. By extrapolation, a safe single engine takeoff would be possible; I just had to accept the risk involved.

So, next morning I taxied out at maximum aircraft weight to demonstrate a single-engine take-off (fingers crossed!). The profile to be covered was to start the take-off with both engines roaring at maximum power, accelerate to a stipulated 'decision speed' on the runway, then switch off the right engine, and thereafter accelerate on single engine till the take-off speed was reached, and then get airborne and climb at that speed. The minimum climb gradient had to be 1.6 per cent. This translates into a climb rate of around 200 feet per minute, which of course is very shallow; but meets the stipulated minimum obstacle clearance requirement.

I carried out the take-off as per the profile, switching off the right engine at 95 knots speed while still on the runway, then accelerating on single engine till the take-off speed of 113 knots, and getting airborne and climbing away at that speed. The climb was timed and the gradient worked out to 1.8 per cent which was more than the stipulated minimum of 1.6 per cent. I was greatly relieved that a risky test like this, which I was doing for the first time, had been successfully accomplished, and had proved the aircraft's airworthiness.

Now, the ICPA had no way of justifying the strike. But as a desperate measure, they took a stand that the single-engine take-off looked risky. Of course it was a risky test, but acceptable as per International Safety Standards. The whole matter was then taken to court. Two eminent lawyers were appointed by the government to defend the aircraft's airworthiness – one was Soli Sorabji (who later became Attorney General) and Ashok Sen (later to become Law Minister). I had to attend the court as a primary witness in this whole episode. I also had the onerous task of explaining the technical intricacies of single-engine take-off on the Avro to the two eminent lawyers, both of whom were not inclined to pay much attention to a young Squadron Leader! I did my best and they managed to get the basics of the take-off profile in order to present their arguments in court. The ICPA made their lawyers argue that Sqn. Ldr. Ashoka's reports on the aircraft's performance could not be trusted, as he was an interested party. The judge (Justice Tulzapurkar), a cool person, shot back that there was no evidence whatsoever to doubt Sqn. Ldr. Ashoka's integrity as the performance figures were fully transparent and totally valid. Then he read out his concluding judgement which cleared all doubts about the Avro's airworthiness. Thus came to an end a period of great turmoil for me as well as for HAL.

Around this time, the Directorate General of Civil Aviation(DGCA) thought it necessary to study the single-engine take-off performance of Avro in greater detail. The scientific community too was eager to lay their hands on thorough technical scrutiny of the matter. Consequently, a committee was formed under the chairmanship of Dr. Satish Dhawan who was at that time the Director of Indian Institute of Science (IISc), Bangalore, to probe deeper into the matter. It was decided that more data needed to be collected on the single-engine take-offs at max. weight on two Avro aircraft – one, a new aircraft off the production line at HAL Kanpur, and another, an in-service aircraft from Indian Airlines. Ten single engine take-offs were to be done on each of these aircraft. These were very risky tests, since even a one off strong down current of air after take-off could cause a crash. However, as a Test Pilot, taking risks was a part of my job, and I had to stick to my dharma.

But unlike the test in Bombay, this time there was thorough preparation and support. I ended up doing these 20 single-engine take-offs on the two aircraft, at maximum weight – and all at Kanpur airfield. Fortunately for me, we had no problem. All data was recorded onboard, to provide good bit of home work for the scientific committee. In the bargain, I qualified myself as the only pilot, at least in India, to complete so many single engine take-offs on a two-engine transport aircraft, and that too at maximum weight.

Scientists have a voracious appetite for data, which they can analyse in depth and draw some useful conclusions. The data collected from these single-engine take-offs whetted their appetite for more. But now they wanted data not on single engine, but on NO engine! If the aircraft could be put into a descent with both engines switched off, the ensuing descent rate at a given speed would enable accurate calculation of aerodynamic drag. I was thus given this exciting task. I felt that fitting an additional battery for in-flight re-start of the engines was necessary, as with both engines off, all electrical services would run solely on the existing battery, thus draining it and possibly putting engine re-start in jeopardy.

This modification done, I would switch off both engines at the required height and carry out steady descents at constant speed. All the data was recorded on board. This was done successfully over a few flights and a mass of data given to the scientists for their analysis. On the last flight, I thought that as I would never again get a chance to switch off both engines in the air, why not carry out a landing with both engines off, as a befitting finale. So, before joining circuit for landing, I switched off both engines and called up finals for landing. The aircraft glided silently and gracefully and I had no problem making a good landing. I even managed to taxi back to the parking area with both engines still off, the ground crew staring in disbelief at such a silent arrival! The scientists were duly satiated with the data and no more radical tests were suggested thereafter. I ended up with one more record under my belt.

Paratrooping and Supply Dropping Trials

In early 1972, one Avro aircraft (No. 1176) had been modified for paratrooping and supply dropping roles. For this, the small passenger door at the rear end on the left side of the fuselage had been removed and replaced with a large sliding door. The trials had to first determine whether the paratrooper(or the load) that exited through this door, had adequate clearance from the tailplane, which was in close proximity. Also, we had to check if the slip stream of the left engine caused any problem through turbulence. These were factors which could be determined only by actual drops by paratroopers. An expert British team had been called upon to guide us during these trials. We had detailed discussions on the conduct of the trials, and it was decided to initially use paratrooper dummies to ensure that adequate clearance was available from the tail plane. For this purpose, the drops would be photographed from an IL-14 transport aircraft, which would flew alongside in close formation. And, once the dummy drops were proven to be safe, live drops could be undertaken.

I flew the aircraft down to IAF Station Agra, which operated Paratroopers' Training school (PTS) and had a delineated dropping zone(DZ) nearby where we were to conduct the trials. Initially, I dropped the dummies and photographs were taken from the IL-14 aircraft. These were scrutinised in detail to establish safe clearance from the tailplane. Once this was done, the first live jump was done by an expert Squadron Leader of the Royal air force, a veteran of such trials. He was very happy with the drop and cleared other personnel for the same. We slowly increased the number of paratroopers to be dropped in one run, and ended up finally dropping 30 fully equipped paratroopers in one go. All of them found the drops very comfortable and safe. I had to allow for the wind effect as well as the distance the aircraft would travel in the process of all the 30 paratroopers clearing the aircraft, to ensure that they all landed within the DZ. Here, my experience with bombing on fighters helped and all landed on target, within the DZ.

For the supply dropping role, the aircraft was modified with a rail system inside the fuselage, over which the loads would roll down, and get ejected through the large door on the left side. The loads were packed in large wooden crates with small wheels to roll over the rails. The maximum load that the aircraft could accommodate was eight cases of 1,000 pounds each. I had to work out a flying technique where at the appropriate moment, I opened full power and got into a relatively steep climbing attitude to make the loads roll down the rails to get ejected. The timing for this had to be precise. We worked this out through trial and error, and finally had an efficient and successful working system. We carried out all these trials at the same DZ in Agra, where we had done the paratrooping trials. Once this was over, we were ready to go for the real supply drops in the operational areas of J&K and Ladakh, and later in the north eastern sector.

Pathankot was the IAF base for supply dropping sorties into J&K. The IAF was operating C-119 Packet aircraft on a daily basis for supply dropping and we joined in with our Avro to supplement the effort, while concurrently also carrying out our trials. The IAF provided me with a co-pilot who was familiar with the area to help me navigate in the mountainous region and locate the dropping zones. Maps were not of any great use here, and one had to have physical experience of the area before embarking on such flights. I carried out a number of flights to drop loads at Niru, Turtok and Chalunka. These DZs were located on some clearings on the side of a hill or on the banks of streams flowing through narrow valleys. The DZs were mostly small in size and demanded an accurate drop by the pilot. Luckily for me, our drops were pretty accurate and the army personnel were able to retrieve most of the loads.

After completing the trials in J&K, I flew the aircraft down to Leh in Ladakh to carryout trial drops at Sasoma, Fukche and TSogsalu DZs. Leh airfield is situated at a height of 11,000ft and the atmospheric pressure there is around 9.7 psi as against the sea level pressure of 14.7psi. Consequently, it requires some acclimatisation to feel comfortable. I landed there along with my crew on Sept.22, 1972 a little before the onset of winter. It was already quite cold and one could feel some lightness in the head on account of the thin air. We were administered oxygen and advised to rest a little to gradually acclimatise. As the day ended, an intensely bright moon came up over the horizon, the barren hills starkly etched against the spotless sky, and it was a sight to remember. One encounters such sights often in the course of flying, and one cannot but be deeply moved by it, provided one has a sensitive enough eye, and a soft enough heart!

Over the next two days, we carried out drops which were pretty challenging. Some of these DZs were at 16,000 to 17,000ft, and when the door was opened for the drop, the low atmospheric pressure and the sub-zero wind blast were pretty unnerving for the crew positioned there. They were, of course, secured with ropes tied to their waists, and also had to, by turns, get hold of an oxygen mask which was hung in that area and take a few deep inhalations. It was a fight against the elements. We were not quite prepared for it and had to innovate as we went along.

These dropping zones in the Ladakh region are located in narrow valleys, flanked by sheer rock faces on either side, extending a good 1,000ft or more above our flight path. Because of the narrow space available in the gorge, it was not considered safe to attempt turning the aircraft around at will, and you were forced to continue straight ahead following the valley, till you came to the junction of a tributary. Here you have sufficient space to turn around safely and exit the valley by retracing your path. In these mountains, cloud formations could sometimes descend into the valley quite abruptly, blocking your path. Since the valley is too narrow to permit entering cloud and climbing without visual contact with the surrounding rock faces, or to turn around, you could get stuck in a death trap with no escape route-a real rocky dead end!(Pun intended).

I thought I must explore the possibility of turning the Avro around through 180° in that limited space, to escape to safety by retracing our path. I had a hunch that the Avro could do it. So, the next day, after finishing the drop, I decided to give it a try. I reduced speed to 120 knots, and lowered some flap to enable a tighter turn. Then, I decided to get as close as possible to the rock face on my right side so as to create greater space to the left to turn the aircraft around. Now, we judge our distance from an object accurately only when we have some idea of its size. In the case of a flat rock surface, such as we encountered, you have no well-defined object as such, and hence it is impossible to judge your distance from it accurately. The only solution, I thought, was to choose a point on the rock face and start gradually edging in towards it, keeping a check on how fast you are moving in relation to that point. When you find that the rate of movement corresponds roughly to your speed, you are pretty close. When I focussed my eyes on to a spot on the rock, I noticed that I was barely moving in relation to it! Obviously, I was too far. This enabled me to move closer and closer till the spot appeared to move at a reasonable rate. When I looked to the left, I found enough space to turn around. I carried out a steep 180 degree turn to the left quite safely with space to spare. I was mighty pleased that the Avro would not be trapped in case clouds happened to block the path ahead, and hence safe operations would be possible in these mountains. Of course the pilots would have to be briefed appropriately.

In November 1972, I took the aircraft for supply dropping trials to the Eastern sector. I had to carry out supply drops at Naga Hills, NEFA (now Arunachal Pradesh) and Mizo Hills, bordering Burma. These were much smaller hills and the dropping zones were again very small. I first flew the aircraft to Guwahati, and then to Jorhat. From there, we carried out drops at Naga Hills. The next day we flew down to Mohanbari and carried out drops in NEFA. Finally, for drops at various DZs in the Mizo hills, we had to position the aircraft at Kumbhigram. Jorhat acted as our base, so we had to fly from there to Kumbhigram, carry out the drops in Mizo hills and then get back to Jorhat before nightfall. So far our drops had gone off quite well and we did not face the sort of problems encountered in the Himalayas. However, there was another type of unforeseen event awaiting us.

On November 14, 1972, we positioned the aircraft at Kumbhigram to carry out two flights from there to various DZs in the Mizo Hills area, and then return the same day to Jorhat. Kumbhigram had a rather primitive airstrip with no runway lighting, and even more primitive Air traffic services. We landed there in the morning and the ground crew got down to loading up the aircraft. Due to inadequate ground facilities, the flights got delayed and by the time we finished and got ready for the return flight to Jorhat, it was well past sunset. Being winter in the hills, it had turned dark quite early. The Air traffic control had promptly packed up at sunset, and left us to fend for ourselves. No runway lighting, and now, no Air traffic control either! We were left with no option but to get airborne as quickly as possible. So, I started up, taxied out and lined up on the runway with landing lights on. As I started rolling with full power, I could see some 100 yards or so ahead with the landing lights, which was enough to make a safe take-off. However, somewhere around halfway on the take-off run, when we had not quite achieved our takeoff speed, I saw directly in front of us, a large herd of buffaloes lazily crossing the runway. My heart must have stopped for a second; but apparently, my subconscious mind was fully alert. If I abandoned take-off, I would have a lot of buffalo flesh and blood all over, and a crippled aircraft in the midst. I had literally no time to think, and as a reflex, I lowered full flaps, and just as I was about to plough into the flock, I heaved back on the stick hoping that the aircraft could hop over the flock without stalling on to it, and may be thump down on the other side. There was no guarantee that it would work, but I had no choice. Luck was, however, in our favour, and we just managed to clear the flock, touched gently on the other side and got airborne again – a really narrow escape!

When we were established into a steady climb, a hot cup of coffee was brought up to the cockpit by one of the technicians, as per the standard practice, all on board being totally oblivious of the scary happenings. I put the aircraft into Auto pilot, eased my straps, and took a hearty swig. Coffee never tasted better!

Testing Limits

Sometimes, in flying, when exuberance and aggressiveness are not properly contained, a young pilot can be tempted to overlook the established norms of flying discipline and safety. In aviation parlance, such actions are termed as over confidence. However, when aggressiveness is matched with calculation and skill, new frontiers may be explored. Of course, I do not recommend such actions to anyone.

On fighters like Hunter, Mystere, Gnat, Jaguar and MiG 21, I had carefully practiced 'zoom' takeoffs, which look very impressive. For this, one has to hold the aircraft close to the runway after getting airborne, gather as much speed as possible within the runway length, and then sharply pitch up into a steep climb. Since the climb is steep, the speed falls off quite rapidly, and one has to be alert to ensure that it does not lead to a stall. The way I ensured this was to bank the aircraft by 90° at the right moment in the zoom and let it slide down sideways on to the horizon to regain speed and level flight. The catch here is to judge the exact moment when the bank must come on. This is a matter of judgement and practice and herein lies the possibility of getting into trouble. Of course, one could play safe and not make the climb too steep. But if you want to make it spectacular, you need to get close to the limits. I am proud of the fact that I could do so without problem on most aircraft I have flown, including a transport aircraft like the Avro.

During my operation from Jorhat for supply dropping trials on the Avro, one day I carried out a zoom take-off as described above. That evening when I was at the mess bar, a group of young pilots from the Hunter squadron there came up to me and expressed their desire to watch my take-off from close quarters, and asked me if I could please demonstrate the same on my next flight. So the next day when I lined up for take-off, I saw a number of those pilots positioned on either side of the runway to watch the fun. I carried out the take-off, retracted the undercarriage very low, and kept really close to the runway for some length, then zoomed up in a steep climb and winged-over to head for my sector. The ATC simply transmitted on the radio, "That was hot". I felt gratified that I could impress a fighter base with my lumbering, sedate Avro, and in a domain belonging essentially to fighter aircraft.

When I was a young pilot, in my fighter squadron we would have some kind of a competition as to who could carry out the lowest retraction of the wheels (that is undercarriage retraction) at take-off. This looks quite breathtaking to those watching the take-off. It is a test of one's judgement and finesse in aircraft handling. The danger of course is of the aircraft belly touching the runway surface in the process, a serious matter. I somehow got drawn into a league of pilots who dared to do so, and managed to get pretty proficient at it. Then, I heard some senior pilots talking of 'brush' take-offs, done by some ace pilots on the Spitfire fighter aircraft. These are take-offs where the undercarriage is retracted so low that the wheels actually brush lightly against the runway surface in the process of retracting, making it appear as if the aircraft is getting airborne on account of the wheels being retracted. It is, obviously, as low as it can possibly get, and hence, as spectacular as possible. Of course, also very risky.

I noticed that the Avro was exceptionally steady after take-off. I could hold the aircraft close to the runway and safely carryout a really low undercarriage retraction. I also happened to notice that just prior to getting airborne, there was a slight clicking vibration on the undercarriage lever. I figured that this must be because of the 'chattering' of the electrically operated safety lock, in the process of being withdrawn. The purpose of the safety lock is to ensure that when the aircraft is on the ground and the oleos (or shock absorbers) are compressed due to aircraft weight, the undercarriage cannot be retracted. This is a safety requirement to prevent inadvertent undercarriage retraction on ground. But on take-off, as one approaches take-off speed, the aircraft is progressively lifted up, reducing the pressure on the oleos and the wheels. The oleos, therefore, extend. At a specific degree of extension, an electric circuit is activated, which withdraws the safety lock, thus enabling the undercarriage to be retracted after getting airborne, which of course, is very much required.

It occurred to me that at that precise moment when the safety lock is withdrawn, the wheels would still be in physical contact with the runway surface, but there would be hardly any weight on them! An ideal moment to execute a brush take-off. The aircraft would, of course, need to be held dead steady at that stage to ensure that the belly does not scrape the runway, and spoil everything.

Over the next few days, the possibility of carrying out a brush takeoff on the Avro kept going round and round in my mind. It was a battle royale, with my rational mind holding me back from taking such an unnecessary risk, while my aggressive genes pushing me to go ahead and achieve the near impossible. The genes eventually won! Sorry for that !

So, on a calm day, I started the take-off with full power and at the usual speed, eased the nose wheel off the ground, but held the aircraft nose somewhat lower than normal to gather five knots more speed before getting airborne. As I gently eased the stick further back, the nose came up slightly, and I felt the clicking vibration on the undercarriage lever, with my right hand on it. I promptly pulled the lever up, and heard the nose wheel thumping into its bay, and the main wheels gently rubbing against the concrete as they retracted. I held the aircraft dead steady at that height – it must have been no more than two or three feet above the runway surface, built up some speed and then pulled her up steeply into a climb. Hurrah! I had done a Brush take-off on the Avro. A rare feat, and I was mighty pleased.

At a later date, I carried out some low level aerobatics on the MiG 21 for a Hindi film named Silsila, where too I carried out a brush take-off which was filmed.

The fact that the Avro could carry out a steep zoom climb after take-off, made me wonder if it could be made to do a loop (i.e. a vertical circle). This is a basic aerobatic manoeuvre done routinely on trainer and fighter aircraft and is no big deal. But a transport aircraft like the Avro is not designed for it. Its structure is not strong enough to withstand the aerodynamic loads which aerobatic manoeuvres impose. It was again a bit of madness which made me consider the possibility of carrying out a loop on it. The structure of the Avro was designed for a limit load of only 2.5g,

Aerobatic aircraft would have a g limit far in excess of 2.5g. A modern fighter aircraft has, typically, a limit of 8g or more, hence can execute very tight manoeuvres at high speeds. Transport aircraft like the Avro are not required to perform such manoeuvres, and hence have a lower g limit. This saves structural weight.

In a loop, you dive the aircraft to a reasonably high speed, then pitch the nose up continuously to perform a vertical circle. In this process, the speed keeps falling while zooming up, since you are going against gravity. Thus, to ensure that you have enough speed to reach the top of the loop, one needs to pitch up *tightly,* to make a relatively small circle. But a low 'g' limit of 2.5g does not permit a tight pitch up. Herein lies the real problem. It is virtually impossible to establish theoretically whether such a manoeuvre would be feasible within the stipulated g limit of 2.5 g. The only way is to actually try it out. But going straight for a vertical loop could be tempting fate a bit too much. If the speed drops too fast and too much on the upward path, one could get into a stall and even spin – something to be avoided like the plague.

So I decided to carry out a number of climbing turns at 2.5 g at full power, initially putting the aircraft nose 15 to20 degrees above the horizon, and progressively reaching up to 45 degrees above the horizon. This way, I would have the option to abandon the manoeuvre anytime I found it not working out. And once I felt confident enough that it could go around safely in a loop, I could go ahead and take a shot at it. The last step in establishing limit boundaries in aircraft manoeuvres is always a leap into the unknown. One has no choice but to rely on one's judgement to pull it off. And there is never 100 per cent guarantee that it would work. To that extent it is brazenly courting risk. But the only way to push the boundaries is to push it!

So, one day when I took off with low weight for aft- C.G. tests, I first completed the stipulated tests and decided to attempt a loop. As planned, I carried out many dives and climbing turns at 2.5g, progressively getting the climb angle to reach around 45 degrees above the horizon. The rate at which the aircraft could be pitched up at 2.5g,and the rate of drop of speed, gave me confidence that the aircraft would be able to go round in a complete loop.

So in the next dive I went up to a speed of 250 knots, and pulled the aircraft in the vertical plane at a *constant* 2.5g. Initially, the pitch rate was slow in order not to exceed 2.5 g, but as the speed dropped to below 180Knots, I could tighten the pitching, and we were going round nicely. As the speed dropped to 130 Knots or so, I had to reduce the 'g' progressively to ensure that the aircraft does not stall. We made it to the top of the loop at a speed of 105 knots, which was reasonably comfortable. I heaved a sigh of relief that we had made it; little realizing that there were yet some anxious moments in store. As the nose dropped below the horizon, I throttled back both engines to idle power to get maximum drag from propellers, so that the speed does not build up too rapidly towards the limit. Although I maintained 2.5 g accurately in the ensuing steep dive, the speed built up much faster than I had expected. This caused the rate of recovery from the dive at 2.5 g rather slow, which in turn caused the speed to increase faster still– a kind of vicious circle, preventing a quick recovery. Anyway, I managed to recover by 270 Knots. This was below our flight test limit of 290 knots, but pretty close to an uncomfortable trap.

After recovering from the dive, I pulled the aircraft up for another loop to try and improve on the manoeuvre. This time I was more careful, and was able to recover by 240 knots or so, which was much more comfortable.

A loop on the Avro! Tricky but manageable, and all within the aircraft's limits. However, I swore never to push the Avro into it again. It was just not fair.

The production flight test schedule of the Avro called for a specific test to check if the ailerons tend to lock at the fully deflected position at a speed approaching 155 knots on account of over-balance. I noticed that when full aileron was applied at say 140-150 knots, the rolling rate was superb for a transport aircraft. This made me wonder if one could carry out a full roll on it.

A roll is like the movement of a screw driver when it is rotated through 360°. While there is no structural strength problem here, there is the problem of imposing negative 'g' when passing through the inverted position. This is not permissible on the Avro as its systems are not designed for negative 'g' manoeuvres. However, it is possible to apply a small positive 'g' while rolling, which would make the aircraft 'barrel', that is, describe a path like the wire coiling in a spring. This would ensure that no negative g occurs. Such a manoeuvre, is called 'barrel roll', and is routinely carried out on trainer and fighter aircraft. I felt that the Avro would be able to manage such a manoeuvre.

So on one of my flights, I put the aircraft into a dive from 5,000ft altitude, and at 180 knots, pulled the nose up gently above the horizon while rapidly banking to the left. As the speed dropped to 150 knots, I applied full left aileron while keeping a slight backward pressure on the stick to avoid any negative 'g'. The aircraft rolled beautifully through 360°, with the nose dropping a little below the horizon, as we got back to level flight. It turned out to be far easier than I had expected.

Thus the Avro, a 44 seat transport aircraft, earned the distinction (in private circles) of being *fully aerobatic*. God bless the machine!

I would sometimes carry out some low flying in the Avro, towards the end of the flight. For this, I often chose the Ganga's river bed. The river ran pretty close to the eastern edge of the airfield boundary, and had a stretch of some 15 miles towards the southeast, where the river bed was very wide with a number of small sandy islands on it. These islands were full of a tall grass with fluffy tops, a most inviting sight for some real low runs. I had surveyed the stretch thoroughly to ensure that there were no wires running across – a real danger for low flying aircraft. I could then get right down to shake the fluffy tops, with 100 per cent concentration!

The part of the river closest to the runway had raised banks, some 20 ft or so above the water level. From time to time, when Runway 27 (pointing west) was in use, I would fly in low along the river bed from southeast, a bit *below* the deep banks, and approach the field unseen. I would then zoom up and call up on final approach for landing. ATC were initially surprised to see the aircraft abruptly appearing on final approach, but in due course, learnt to enjoy the drama. These were silly tricks, a bit of fun and fooling around.

In December 1972, it was decided to take one Avro aircraft from the production line, to the original designers of the aircraft – Hawker Siddeley, in the UK. The idea was to carry out some performance comparisons between the aircraft produced in Kanpur, and those manufactured in the UK. I was lucky to have Sqn. Ldr. P.M. Ramachandran to help me with the ferry. He was a Test Pilot with a lot of test flying experience on the AVRO, and was also a good friend of mine.

We took off on New Year's Day 1973 from Kanpur and headed across the Arabian sea and landed at a place called Seeb in Muscat. From there we routed through Bahrain, Baghdad, Beirut, Athens, Rome and Paris, and arrived at Woodford, UK on 11th Jan. We had night halts at Beirut, Athens, Rome and Paris and greatly enjoyed our outings. The aircraft behaved well throughout, except on one occasion when we landed at Rome. In the Avro, there is a safety lock on the propellers, which ensures that in the air, the propeller pitch will not go below 16°, as below this angle the propeller drag could increase enormously, causing serious controllability problems. However, after landing, we want the maximum drag from the propellers, so that our landing distance is reduced as much as possible. To enable this, a lever is provided just behind the throttles, which when pulled back removes this lock, enabling the propeller angle to reduce to zero degrees to maximise the propeller drag. However, after we landed at Rome, the propeller stop on one of the propellers did not get withdrawn, even though the lever was pulled back. This meant that the propeller stayed at 16 deg. In this condition, when the throttle is subsequently opened to taxy, the 16° angle of the propellers would offer a much higher rotational drag, causing the turbine temperature to shoot up beyond its limits. I had to switch off the engine and taxy back on single engine, which was not really a problem. The real worry, of course, was to detect the cause of the problem and to rectify it in time, so as not to disrupt our itinerary.

Luckily, when the ground crew checked the system, they detected a faulty micro-switch. A replacement rectified the problem and we were back on line. Next day we took off for Paris and landed there for an overnight halt. On the last leg from Paris to Woodford, UK, there was a complete cloud cover under us and we could not see the ground or the English Channel at all. However, the radar at Woodford spotted us, and guided us perfectly on to final approach for landing. We landed safely, bringing to an end an enjoyable international safari.

Gliders: Rohini and Ardhra

During my stay at HAL Kanpur, in addition to the Avro, two types of gliders (i.e. sailplanes) were also being produced – one was the Rohini two-seater, and the other was the single seat Ardhra. While the Rohini had been certified earlier, we had to put the Ardhra through the full certification testing. Since this required clearing it for spin recovery among other tests, we had to climb to a higher altitude to carry out the tests.

Therefore, we had to use an aero-tow by an aircraft, as a winch launch could take us up to only 500-700 ft, which was not sufficient for spinning. An Auster IX light aircraft was used to tow us up to 3,000ft or so. We would then release the tow and carry out stalls, followed by two turn spins to left and right, then dive it to its maximum speed to check the control feel, carry out one or two loops and return for landing. All in one mad rush, as without an engine you are continuously losing height.

Once the certification bit of flying on the Ardhra was over and the glider came out on production line, we used the winch for the launch, as spinning tests were not required to be done any more. We would wait for some 5 or 6 gliders to get ready for flight testing, and then arrange for a half day of gliding from the shoulders of the runway. The winch would get us up to around 600ft altitude. After releasing the cable, if there was no possibility of an up current, we needed to hurry through our flight tests – a quick stall, a high-speed dive and a loop, and immediately position for a landing. However, if you spotted a thermal (up current) close by, indicated by a flock of birds spiralling up, you were in luck, and could well get a free ride up to 3,000 to 4,000ft. With no engine to make a noise, the only sound you hear is that of the wind. There is a great sense of peace in this kind of flying. Also, once you are up at a reasonable height, you can take your own time to complete the test schedule, and enjoy the scenery.

Sometimes, however, the kites (eagles) do not take kindly to an intruder. On one occasion, a kite that was flying alongside, virtually in close formation to our glider, tried to attack the glider with claws drawn out menacingly. I had to waggle my wings to get rid of him. A large kite can easily damage the soft fabric of the glider with its claws and create a big problem. Mostly, however, they don't mind some company, but this one was belligerent, and rather possessive of its piece of sky. With some justification, I guess.

Most of these gliders have just one small wheel centrally located under the belly, somewhere in the middle of its length, and a convex skid under the nose. After landing, the pilot has to push the stick forward to rub the skid against the ground to provide braking effect. Once the glider comes to a halt, the ailerons would become ineffective, and one wing tip would go down and rest on the ground. During launch, the ground crew, one on each side, would hold the wings level and run along the glider till the glider gathered some speed to make the ailerons effective enough to keep the wings level. While landing, it was a challenge to touch down precisely at a known point, such that the glider comes to a halt where the ground crew are waiting – so they could grab the wing tip before it went down to the ground. With some experience, I was able to do so most of the time. These were some simple challenges of glider flying. And great fun too!

Supersonics

HINDUSTAN AERONAUTICS LTD, NASIK

Mach 2 Fighters: Mig-21 & the Sukhoi 7

By late 1974, I had spent over seven years flight testing and pushing the Avro at HAL Kanpur. I had thoroughly enjoyed flirting with it but wanted to get back to my original love of flying fighter aircraft. As the MiG 21 was by then in full production at HAL Nasik, I requested for a transfer to that Division, which came through quickly. I arrived at Ojhar Township (HAL Nasik) in April '75 with my family, and settled down in an independent villa-like house with a lovely garden. It was a welcome change from congested Kanpur, to the fresh and clean Ojhar township. It was also a pleasant challenge to be the Chief Test Pilot at a factory producing the celebrated Mach 2 fighter, the first truly supersonic fighter on Indian soil. I was highly motivated and impatient to befriend this elegant machine.

The MiG 21 was a really beautiful aircraft. Its triangular delta wings and the well crafted sleek lines were a thrill to watch. It was the first fighter of the IAF to have an afterburner (or reheat) system on its engine – a standard feature on supersonic fighters. In this system, additional fuel is injected into the exhaust gases that are passing through the jet pipe after combustion, and re-ignited. Since these gases still contain some unused oxygen, a big flame is created in the jet pipe, which results in further accelerating the gases. This causes an increase in thrust by over 50 per cent. Obviously, the aircraft's performance gets a big boost. There is, however, a rather heavy penalty to be paid in terms of fuel consumption, and the pilot has to be economical in its usage.

Whenever afterburner is used, the exhaust nozzle at the rear end has to open up to permit easy flow of the much larger volume of gases generated. For this purpose, a hydraulically operated variable nozzle system is provided. This system automatically regulates the diameter of the nozzle aperture in accordance with the mass flow of the exhaust gases, to ensure engine stability. In slower aircraft, a fixed air intake in front is adequate, but for supersonic flight the intake geometry and it's capture area have to be variable. This ensures that the quantity of airflow coming through the intake is regulated to match with the capacity of the engine to handle it. This is necessary because the airflow through the intake increases enormously in supersonic flight, and hence needs to be controlled. In addition, the shock waves formed at the intake in supersonic flight, also need to be optimally placed for maximum pressure recovery and engine stability. In the MiG 21 both these objectives are met with great precision by an ingenious device - a moving cone located right in the centre of the circular air-intake, with its apex pointing straight ahead. Forward and aft movement of this cone changes the air intake aperture area to regulate the quantum of air flow coming on to the compressor. And, the contour of the cone surface ensures optimum placement of shock waves at the intake. The cone itself is moved hydraulically and is fully automatic in its operation.

The flight controls of the MiG 21 were simple in design and very reliable. For pitch control, there was a single large all-moving horizontal stabilizer (a large elevator) at the tail end, which was moved hydraulically, with no provision for manual operation. The ailerons (for roll control) were hydraulically powered, but also had provision for manual operation. The rudder, however, was totally manually operated, with no hydraulic power – something surprising for a Mach 2 fighter. The Russian design philosophy of 'keeping it simple' was evident. The point to note is that simplicity does not undermine effectiveness and ease of operation, and in fact, enhances reliability.

The MiG 21 was also the first aircraft in IAF to have 'Q' feel system in its longitudinal flight control. The letter 'Q' stands for dynamic air pressure, which is proportional to aircraft speed. All slow speed aircraft with manual controls, provide a natural 'Q' feel to the pilot, since he directly feels the air pressure against which he pushes the control surface by moving the stick. However, in aircraft having hydraulically powered flight controls, the pilot does not feel the air pressure at all, since it is the hydraulic jack that moves the control surface. He is, however, provided with an artificial spring feel system, which provides some feel, as larger control movements require larger forces against the spring. Aircraft like Mystere, Hunter, and Gnat all had such artificial feel systems in the flight controls. But these did not provide adequate protection against over-sensitivity at high speeds. Consequently, over-controlling remained a distinct possibility at high speeds. My experience of the un-controlled oscillations on the Mystere proved the point.

The 'Q' feel system on the MiG 21 was far more advanced and provided optimal control sensitivity to the pilot under all conditions of fight, throughout the aircraft's speed range from 300 kmph to 1300 kmph and up to Mach 2.1 at high altitudes. Speed and altitude sensors were used to determine what level of sensitivity was desirable. On that basis, the geometry of the control system linkages was altered to achieve the desired result. It was essentially a mechanical system, and proved to be trouble-free, a great boon to the MiG 21 pilot.

The later models of Mig 21 had what is called Blown flaps, which I had first encountered on the Scimitar naval fighter at ETPS. However, on the MiG 21, this downward jet of air over the flaps causes a nose down pitching of the aircraft just prior to touch down, requiring the pilot to quickly bring the stick back a little to get a smooth touchdown. Of course, the pilots get used to this quite easily. It was a useful system, and made landing that much more relaxed, at a lower speed.

The wheel brake system on the MiG 21 worked on Pneumatic (i.e. air) pressure. There were two novel features of this system. Firstly, the system was not charged by any on-board compressor, as was normally the case on other aircraft. Instead, it was provided with a ground-charged bottle, with no provision for charging in the air. There was thus, a limited supply of compressed air available to the pilot for using brakes during taxying out for take-off, and subsequently, for braking on landing and taxying back. Initially, I felt a bit uncomfortable with the limited supply of air. However, with a little practice at economy, it was quite manageable. This little care demanded of the pilot saved a lot of weight and complexity. The other novel aspect of the system was that braking was provided on all three wheels, unlike other aircraft, where it was available only on the two main wheels. Having brakes on the nose wheel as well, made for a significant increase in deceleration after landing, resulting in shorter landing distance. Of course, the nose wheel brake had to be selected off for taxying on ground to facilitate turning. The system was altogether simple, effective and pilot friendly.

Initial models of MiG 21 were optimized for supersonic radar interception at high altitudes, and could carry just two air-to-air missiles, one under each wing. In addition, there was a belly station where you could carry a 490 litre fuel tank or a 23mm gun pack. The later models of the aircraft had a built in 23mm gun in the front fuselage, and had two stations under each wing for weapons and fuel tanks. The belly station could carry a large 800 litre fuel tank. Thus, these later models had better range and weapons capability, and hence were far more effective in ground attack role, while retaining Radar interception capability.

The earlier model of the MiG 21 had a simple autopilot, which was mainly for emergency, in case the pilot got disoriented. In such a case, he just had to press a red button on his stick, and the aircraft would automatically bring itself to the wings-level condition. However, there was no control in the pitching plane. It was, nevertheless, a great help to the pilot. The later models of the aircraft had a full-fledged autopilot, which had full control in pitch also. In these aircraft, when the emergency (levelling) button was pressed, the aircraft would not only go to wings level position, but the nose of the aircraft would also be pitched up or down to bring it to a perfect straight and level flight at constant altitude. This was a great device to help the pilot, especially if he was disabled in flight for any reason. In one instance, a squadron pilot happened to suffer from some serious medical problem in the air, and went into a semi-conscious state. He quickly pointed the aircraft towards the base and pressed the levelling button on the stick. The aircraft flew perfectly in level flight for some 10 minutes, when the pilot woke up and found himself close to the base! In the absence of this device, we could have lost the pilot as well as the aircraft.

The radar on the MiG 21 could detect a target up to a range of 50 km, and guide the pilot to bring him within missile firing range of 10km or less, and give him the command to fire the missile. All this was done through clear and bold images on the radar screen and well-timed commands – a difficult task made commendably easy for the overworked fighter pilot.

I must mention some interesting aspects of the MiG 21's cockpit. In most Western designed aircraft, the cockpits are very neat-looking and aesthetically appealing, with switches and controls for various systems placed in neat groupings and perfect lines like army columns. In comparison, the MiG 21 cockpit looked rather haphazard. The switches and controls were in small groups scattered all over the cockpit, but with a certain practical logic, which gave them a unique character, and made them easy to locate and operate. It was a rustic horse-sense type of arrangement, possibly lacking in aesthetics, but extremely pilot-friendly and effective. The design of the throttle needs a special mention. It was a beautifully machined component, which moved from fuel off position at the rear, to maximum afterburner position when fully forward. It moved in a delightful progression of clicks and catches, which enabled the pilot to operate it accurately, even with eyes closed. In fact, I would often operate it over its entire range a couple of times before starting the engine, just to enjoy the precision of its design. All cockpit controls also had a firm and solid feel, and all switches operated with a positive click. These small things made a big difference to the level of pilot comfort.

Testing

The HAL factory at Ojhar, Nasik had two separate lines for aircraft production – one was for manufacture of new aircraft, and another for periodic overhaul of the aircraft already in service with IAF. During my stay at HAL Nasik, three different models of the aircraft came up for test flights. These were MiG-21FL, MiG-21M and MiG-21BIS. Basically, all these models were similar in their performance, but with some differences in their systems. Their flight test schedules were, thus, more or less the same, and essentially comprised of three separate assignments. One flight was required for each assignment. The first assignment was to climb to 13km altitude (about 43,000ft), and to carry out a level acceleration up to its maximum speed of 2.1 Mach, checking aircraft and engine behaviour and performance. The second assignment required a supersonic climb at 1.8 Mach to an altitude of 19 to 20km (about 65,000ft), to check engine stability, and handling characteristics at high altitudes. And the third assignment was to check radar performance. For this last test, two aircraft would get airborne together, each one in turn acting as a target for the other, and carrying out radar interceptions. In addition to these assignments, numerous other checks had to be carried out on the various systems. Thus, an aircraft would, on an average, need around five flights to be cleared. There was usually some spare fuel in each flight to carry out aerobatics and check the aircraft's general handling before coming in to land. Also, in one of the flights, we had to carry out a supersonic run at low altitude to touch the structural limit speed of around 1,200kmph on the FL model and 1,350kmph on the later models. This exposes the aircraft to very high dynamic air pressures.

In the year 1977, we found that most of the overhauled aircraft (with overhauled engines) were not performing as well as earlier. Their supersonic acceleration timings had deteriorated (though meeting the minimum level). At the same time, the engine jet-pipe temperatures had become higher than normal. While these figures were all within the acceptable range, I felt unhappy about the deterioration in performance. There had to be a good reason for such an occurrence now, when we had not experienced it earlier. I spent a lot of time pondering over the phenomenon. If the engine temperature was high, there was obviously not enough airflow through the compressor, resulting in a lower thrust. And to meet the thrust requirement at the test-bed in the engine factory, they would have increased the fuel flow to attain the minimum 'pass' value of thrust. However, this would also result in higher engine temperature, though within limits. We would thus, have precisely the conditions we were faced with – a relatively poor thrust (and hence acceleration), and higher engine temperature. When I thought of lower airflow through compressor, it had to be due to poorer compressor efficiency, which in turn would depend on the aerodynamic efficiency of the compressor blades, similar to my experience on the Avro at Bombay.

I decided to visit the engine factory at Koraput, Orissa to check on this aspect. So, I landed up there and got into a meeting with all the engine experts. When I mentioned the problem, and suggested that the reason could be poorer aerodynamic efficiency of the compressor blades, the instant reaction was that the blades were checked strictly to given standards and there was no question of passing a blade which is not to stipulated standards. As a matter of interest, I asked if they had to resort to some replacements of worn out or corroded compressor blades during overhaul. They said, "Yes, some blades had to be replaced." I asked them to let me know what the rejection rate of these blades was in the three previous years, as compared to 1977. When the data was brought to the table the next day, it could be seen that the number of blades rejected in recent years was much *higher* than in 1977. When queried further, it transpired that, in order to reduce the cost of overhaul, they had decided to minimise rejections and took to 'reworking' the blades, where required, and refitting them. Clearly, the aerodynamic quality of the blades had suffered and was causing our problem. On my insistence, they reverted to the earlier stricter standards. Thereafter, the engines which came after overhaul were cured of this problem. I was gratified that we were able to give our fighter pilots the best performance the aircraft was capable of.

During the supersonic run at low altitudes on the MiG 21 FL model, as mentioned earlier, the test schedule required us to accelerate to 1,200 kmph to check aircraft behaviour. At such high speeds at low altitude, the dynamic air pressure is very high, and can cause distortions in some of the structural parts, resulting in high-frequency vibrations on the aircraft, called 'flutter'. On some aircraft we found this phenomenon setting in as we crossed Mach 1 at low altitudes. The whole aircraft would get into severe vibrations, which could even result in structural failure of some airframe component like a control surface, if allowed to persist. Obviously a serious safety hazard.

When I reported it, I was told that HAL Nasik had obtained a concession from Air HQ to restrict the maximum speed of the aircraft at lower heights to avoid such vibrations. I was shocked that we were putting speed restrictions on a frontline combat aircraft, and felt that it was grossly unfair to our fighter pilots, as it could put them at a severe disadvantage in combat and also create a serious safety hazard. I put my foot down that I would not clear an aircraft with such speed restrictions, and at the same time assured the management that, given some time, we would solve the problem.

That year (1976), five aircraft were held back for this defect, and were not delivered to the IAF. It was then my moral responsibility to help solve the problem. I asked the technical staff to first take one of the five aircraft for rectification, and check all moving surfaces and other components for any play. They checked the same and rectified what they could detect. I got airborne the next day to test the aircraft, and again encountered these vibrations, with no signs of any improvement. I ended up doing some 10 flights like this after some rectification or the other, and every time got into severe vibrations the moment I crossed Mach 1.0 at low altitude. The vibrations were quite frightening, and I hoped I did not lose a control surface in the bargain, which could be fatal at such high speeds. Finally, they removed the ailerons to check if there was anything abnormal in the linkages. And lo and behold, they found excessive wear on one of the aileron bearings – something which could not be detected unless the ailerons were removed. Once this was rectified, the problem vanished, and the aircraft sailed through smoothly right up to 1,200 kmph.

Thereafter, other pending aircraft were rectified in a similar fashion by September that year, and I test flew and cleared all of them one by one. We then dispatched a team to all the MiG 21 squadrons to carry out similar rectification on all aircraft which were earlier cleared under concession. It took a further few months to complete the task, but it was a matter of great satisfaction to finally restore all these aircraft to their original performance level.

In the second assignment of the flight test schedule, as already mentioned, we had to carry out a supersonic climb at 1.8 Mach, to the ceiling altitude of around 65,000 ft, and check engine performance and stability, among other things. We also had to carry out a test to engage afterburner at a low speed of 500 kmph at 50,000 ft, to check that the afterburner lights up and stabilizes satisfactorily. We found that during these two tests, we would sometimes have an engine flame out (engine failure). The aircraft then had to be descended to 25,000 ft to restart the engine. Once we got a successful relight, we would promptly return to base and land. The technical staff would then remove the engine, pack it and send it by rail to the engine factory at Koraput in Orissa for investigation and necessary rectification.

Invariably, the engine would arrive back in HAL Nasik (in a few months time) with a report saying 'no defect detected'. When I became aware of such a situation, I decided to study the matter in detail to establish the possible cause, and to see if we could prevent such flameouts. I got hold of all the old files of aircraft which had experienced engine flame-outs during the process of flight tests, and scrutinised their performance details. I found that all aircraft which had this problem, gave better than normal supersonic acceleration, and had relatively lower engine temperatures. This implied a higher air mass flow through the engine, giving higher thrust and lower engine temperatures. Higher mass flow means higher compressor efficiency, implying higher compression *ratio* across the compressor.

Now, it is a known fact that at very high compression ratios, the compressor tends to 'surge' and stall – in other words it is unable to sustain smooth airflow through the engine, leading to a flame-out. This is on account of the fact that the compressor is made to push air from lower pressure at the air intake, to very high pressure at its delivery side. This, of course, is in stark opposition to the natural law which states that air tends to flow from higher pressure to a lower pressure (just prick an inflated balloon to witness this). Thus, the compressor actually performs an 'uphill' task, pushing air against progressively rising pressures, rightly termed 'adverse pressure gradient'. In this, it has its own limits. Beyond a certain pressure ratio (i.e. adverse gradient), it is unable to push the air smoothly to sustain combustion. When this happens, the airflow gets very disturbed, often causing a flame-out. I felt that, as all engines which flamed out showed higher thrust, we could afford to reduce their thrust a little, while still retaining acceptable levels of acceleration. This would result in reducing compression ratios and making the engine more stable at higher altitudes. All we had to do was to reduce the fuel flow to the afterburner a little, to achieve the desired result. Once this was done, the problem was overcome; and we saved all the time and effort of removing the engine and sending it all the way to Koraput in Orissa, and getting it back, with no clue as to why it flamed out! Common sense always wins!

During my stay at HAL Nasik, I had encountered engine flame-outs on five occasions, mostly around a height of 65,000ft, at a speed of 1.8Mach. The first action by the pilot is to cut off the fuel supply to the engine and switch off all non-essential electrical loads to conserve battery power, which is required for restarting the engine. The aircraft has to be descended to around 25,000ft to provide higher air density, which is required for re-lighting the engine. It is a long glide from 65,000ft to 25,000 ft with a DEAD engine. And a lot of it is at supersonic speeds! Since a dead engine does not suck air like a live engine, excessive air pressure builds up inside the engine air intake channel due to the supersonic speed. This causes big 'bangs' inside the intake, which shakes the aircraft at random, and makes the pilot feel as if something might give way; quite uncomfortable. However, as the speed reduces to subsonic values, these bangs slowly disappear, and the aircraft glides smoothly. Once the altitude reduces to 25,000ft, a relight is attempted at a speed of 500-550kmph. The pilot spends some anxious moments waiting for the RPM and engine temperature to start rising, indicating a successful relight. Once that happens, all electrics are brought on line again and the pilot's worries are over.

However, if the relight is not successful, the pilot has no choice but to eject. On one occasion, when I had such a flame out and attempted a re-light, I found that the engine would not start. I came right down to around 5,000-6,000ft, feverishly trying to re-start it, and was preparing to eject, when the engine slowly picked up, and I managed to land back safely. I could not figure out why on just this occasion it was reluctant to start. On all other occasions, I got a fairly quick relight. I am sure it was to give me a fright, which it sure did !!

The outside air temperature at 65,000 ft is around 100°C below zero, and the atmospheric pressure is just around $1/14^{th}$ of what it is at sea level. If the human body is exposed to such conditions, it would possibly burst like an over-ripe tomato. Of course, inside the cockpit, the air pressure and temperature are maintained at acceptable levels by the pressurization and air conditioning systems. But in case of failure of the systems, or if the canopy gets blown off or cracks for some reason, the pilot would not be able to survive.

In order to protect him against such an eventuality, he has to wear a special pressure suit, whenever he undertakes a very high altitude flight. I had mentioned earlier about a 'g' suit, which all fighter pilots have to wear to minimise the chances of blacking- out in high 'g' manoeuvres. The pressure suit works in a similar fashion, but unlike a 'g' suit which tightens only around the midriff, the pressure suit tightens around the entire body, embracing it in a very tight grip from neck to feet, thus protecting the pilot's body from being exposed to the low pressure. This happens automatically if the air pressure in the cockpit drops below a certain level. The pilot also wears a special helmet, which seals his neck and head against the low pressure. He also wears special gloves which also inflate automatically to protect his fingers. In this attire, he could easily be mistaken for an astronaut. The suit itself is not very comfortable, as it needs to be very tight in order to be effective. A technician has to help you to get into it, and once you have it on, he tightens a whole array of strings to make it super tight. The pilot has to wear special silken inners so that the pressure suit does not prick him over much. It is altogether a bind to get into and out of the pressure suit, but it is also a life-saving device. So no hard feelings!

To execute a supersonic climb to limit altitude, you first climb to 43,000ft, level out and accelerate through Mach 1.0 with full afterburner. The initial acceleration is a bit poor, but as you cross 1.4 Mach, the acceleration is much better, and by 1.8 Mach the aircraft is kind of running away from you. At this Mach number, you pull the aircraft up into a rather steep climb to maintain 1.8 Mach. In spite of a high aerodynamic drag at that speed, the MiG 21 climbs beautifully at the rate of 20,000ft per minute at this high supersonic speed. Thanks to the superb intake design, there is a dramatic increase in airflow to the engine, and hence in its thrust, at these high Mach numbers. It takes just about a minute to climb from 43,000ft to around 65,000ft. As you reach this ceiling height, there is an abrupt reduction in engine noise – something like a deflating balloon, and the thrust drops off significantly. The pilot has to lower the aircraft nose to maintain 1.8 Mach, and he knows that he has almost reached his ceiling height. The reason for this sudden drop in thrust is as follows: As you are climbing up, the air mass flow to the engine reduces due to reduction in the atmospheric pressure and density, causing a steady reduction in thrust. But as you gain height, the outside temperature also keeps dropping, which restores the mass flow to a degree, thus minimizing the drop in thrust. At ceiling height, however, the outside air temperature ceases to drop any further, and stabilises at around minus 100°C. Hence, there is no more any 'restoration' of thrust. This is what causes an abrupt reduction in engine thrust and a drop in climb rate. Anyway, it offers an unmistakable indication that you are close to your ceiling height.

In supersonic flight at high altitude, the flight controls become quite sluggish and the aircraft stability increases significantly. Naturally, aircraft manoeuvrability suffers a great deal. Though you are cutting through the air at about 2000 kmph, the dynamic pressure is equivalent to a sea-level speed of just 500 kmph, due to the thin air. The aircraft response to control inputs is thus quite sluggish, like driving a car over sand or gravel. Not particularly exciting. The thrill, if any, is in seeing the Mach meter needle at Mach 1.8. Of course, there are other pleasures at such a high perch; the dark deep blue of the sky alone may be sufficient compensation. But there is a feeling too, of being far away from it all!! An elevated sense of peace and quiet pervades the cockpit, along with a heightened sense of bonding with the aircraft. A very special sensation, not easy to describe.

One day, when I was carrying out Assignment One, and accelerating through Mach 1.5 at 43,000ft, I heard a loud bang from the engine, and the aircraft got into severe vibrations. The engine temperature also started shooting up rapidly. I immediately throttled back the engine to idle RPM, and called up the ATC to say that I probably had a turbine failure, and may have to eject. I was about 100km from base at that time, and wanted to get as close to base as possible before ejecting, to facilitate early rescue. For this reason, I did not switch off the engine. I knew that there was risk of fire, if there was a fuel leak, and was ready to eject if that showed up. It was my good luck that the fire warning light never came on. As the speed reduced below Mach 1.0, I stabilised the descent at 500kmph. At idle RPM, the vibrations were not too severe, though still worrisome. However, I could not dare to increase power, as it could have instantly caused the problem to escalate. I was losing height at a high rate, and was doubtful of being able to reach the runway. As I came closer to base, however, I realized that I may well be able to reach the runway, and carryout a forced landing. There was, of course, no question of increasing engine power, for fear of triggering a further explosion. I informed the ATC that I would attempt a forced landing on the runway. I arrived on the downwind leg close to the runway at a height of about 10,000ft and lowered the undercarriage and partial flap, and turned on to final approach, keeping a speed of 450 to 500 kmph. I was now committed to land and hoped I make the runway threshold at the correct height and speed and also not overshoot too much. As luck would have it, I was over the threshold at some 10-20 feet. As I flared out, I switched off the engine to avoid any further imbalance in its rotation, which could yet cause some problem. I managed to do a fairly good landing, deployed the brake parachute and came to a stop 500 metres or so from the runway end. I opened the canopy and made my way over the fuselage and onto the left wing and hopped on to the runway. And took a deep breath !!

The news of my emergency had spread, and the Managing Director and General Manager, and other officers had driven over in their cars to meet me. When I narrated the events, I was asked why I did not eject, as there was a real possibility of engine fire, and even an explosion at any moment. I said that I took the risk as I felt I could manage to land safely if I could make the field. Also, that I could have ejected anytime the condition deteriorated at any stage except when on finals for landing. And since I made it safely, my decision was right. Of course, the truth was that I took a big risk, and there was every chance of my not making it safely. But my luck stood by me!

When the aircraft was wheeled into the hangar and the rear fuselage was removed to get access to the engine, we could see that most of the turbine blades were severely damaged and twisted. They found later that one blade had broken off and churned up the whole thing into a mess. It was a miracle that there was no fire or severe explosion. I was indeed lucky.

I had learnt that some Mig -21 pilots had carried out a manoeuvre, where the aircraft speed is dropped to zero by getting her into a steep climb, then pitching the aircraft nose down at an appropriate moment to recover in a dive. In this process, the speed touches the zero mark on top of the manoeuvre. I was quite intrigued by such a manoeuvre, and decided to try it. Of course, there was a possibility of going into a spin. But pitching the nose downwards at the appropriate moment ensures that the aircraft does not reach the stalling angle, and hence is saved from entering into a spin. Still, it needs perfect timing and delicate handling. I started by initially pitching the nose down at a relatively higher speed just to get a feel of the rate at which the speed drops, and then progressively reduced the speed till I got to zero speed on top of the manoeuvre. The aircraft behaved beautifully, and recovered smoothly. It was a great feeling to fly a supersonic Mach 2 fighter down to zero speed. I used to do this often, and got a special kick out of it.

Flying Displays

During my test flying tenure at HAL Nasik as Chief Test Pilot from 1975 to 1983, there were numerous occasions when I had to carryout flying displays over the airfield for the benefit of visiting VIPs. I had practiced a lot for the same, knowing that as the CTP, this responsibility would fall squarely upon my shoulders. The display was essentially a low level aerobatic show. I found that the earliest FL version of MiG 21 aircraft was the most suited for the purpose. For some reason, the handling qualities of the FL were a notch better than those of the later versions. I had earlier experience of such flight displays on aircraft like Hunter, Mystere and Gnat, and knew what was required to impress the audience. There were three things which one had to ensure to make a good display. Firstly, the display had to be tight and close to the viewers, and never out of their comfortable viewing range. Secondly, the manoeuvres must be crisp and swift, with high rates of roll and high 'g' turns. And lastly, the aircraft should make a lot of noise !! All these required the afterburner to be in operation at full power almost throughout the display, with the speeds being on the higher side. This entails pilot's exposure to high 'g's (+6g or more) for relatively long periods. This is extremely stressful and exhausting. A ten minute vigorous display was easily more tiring than say, a swift two km run, or 200 nonstop push ups. But a good display has its own rewards, and the stress is a small price to pay.

The first time I was called upon to carry out a flight display on the MiG 21 was sometime in 1976, a year after I took over as the CTP at HAL Nasik. The annual meeting of the HAL Board of Directors was to be held at HAL Nasik, and my display was programmed as part of 'entertainment' for the occasion. A tent was erected near the ATC building for the visitors. This was near the half way mark of the runway – an ideal spot to watch the display from.

I started up the aircraft some 15 minutes prior to the arrival time of the visitors. After completing all my checks, I taxied out and lined up on the eastern end of the runway. I waited for a radio call from the control tower confirming the arrival of the visitors and clearing me for take-off. The moment I got the call, I opened full throttle, engaged the afterburner and started my take-off roll. I got airborne just in front of the tent and carried out a low undercarriage retraction - holding the aircraft some 4-5 feet off the runway and accelerating. Just as I reached the end of the runway, I pulled her briskly into a steep climb and gained enough height to carry out a wing-over to reverse direction, and point towards the runway, diving to 300 ft and levelling out. As I came over the runway, I carried out two quick rolls, cut in the afterburner, and turned tightly at 6g on to the display area to the north.

Thereafter, I carried out various aerobatic manoeuvres like loops, rolls, wing-overs, and of course, a full 360° steep turn at 6g, all with full afterburner blazing. Finally, I did a few of my favourite vertical rolls. For this, I accelerated to 850Kph and pulled the aircraft to point vertically upwards and performed 3 or 4 rapid rolls, stopping the rolls as the speed dropped to 450kph or so, and looping her out to point vertically downwards, again carrying out rapid rolls. Recovering from the downward rolls, I pulled out to level flight around 500ft above ground. As I accelerated again to 850kph, I pulled her up and did another set of vertical rolls. Thereafter, I lined up for a high speed run over the runway at 200ft. When directly in front of the VIP tent, I whipped her into a 6g left turn, throttling back to idle rpm and positioning on downwind leg for landing. I lowered the undercarriage and flaps at 500kph and carried out a tight curved approach with 60° bank all the way till I lined up with the runway at 20-30 feet above ground, and carried out the landing, streaming the tail parachute soon after touchdown. The whole show must have taken 15 minutes or so. I was thoroughly exhausted with the long high g exposure, but rather pleased with my display.

In the evening, there was a dinner party in the guest house for the VIPs, with a large gathering of senior officers of HAL and their wives. They all greeted me and said they were thrilled with the display. It sure felt great!

The concrete runway at Ojhar ran east-west, and was located on the northern edge of the HAL complex. Looking from the factory on the south side, one would see a vast expanse of grassy shrub-land beyond the runway, with a string of hills at some distance running east-west. The airfield boundary itself took in much of this land, and since it was a rain-deficient region, the grass was mostly brown, and some 3 feet tall in places. The lay of the land seemed to appeal to a rare species of birds called 'Bustard'(watch the spelling, please!), a bit like the Ostrich, but smaller, standing three feet or so in height, and not overly keen to get airborne. On occasion, one or two of them would stray over to the sides of the runway, looking for prey. Once, when I was taxying back from the end of the runway after landing, I spotted an elderly looking bustard to my left. He had a little beard and a very human-like face! He started running to keep pace with the aircraft, turning his head now and again to give me a dirty look!

He was in beautiful brown camouflage to match the grass, and had a most graceful stride. It was a real treat to watch this rare bird up so close.

Sukhoi 7

During my stay at HAL Nasik, I had the opportunity to carry out production test flights on Sukhoi-7 fighter (not to be confused with Sukhoi-30, which came to India much later). This aircraft was being overhauled at No.11 BRD, which was also located at the IAF station at Ojhar, Nasik. They did not have a test pilot for some time, so I offered to do the needful. I had very little experience on the Su-7, but was keen to have a bash at it. I had to study its flight manual and the test schedules and so on, before undertaking the flights, but had no trouble getting into the act.

The Su-7 was a monster of a fighter aircraft, with thick wings, and hardly had the fine lines one expects of a high speed machine. Yet it could sail through to supersonic speeds, thanks to sheer brute force of its enormous engine with afterburner. The one high-speed feature it had was the high sweep back angle of its wings, which must have made up for the high drag due to its thick wings. Its flight controls were of course, hydraulically powered, but were rather heavy in the air, a feature which impaired its manoeuvrability to a degree. In design and technology it appeared to be a bit ancient and crude, but it was a good work horse! The IAF used the aircraft in the ground attack role, for which it was well equipped. It had good weapon carrying capability, with powerful built-in cannon and two weapon stations on each wing. In addition, it carried two fuel drop tanks side by side under the fuselage. It did some good work during the 1971 war with Pakistan, but also suffered a high attrition rate, possibly due to its size and relatively poor agility. Anyway, I enjoyed flying it, since it was quite a unique machine.

When I moved to HAL Nasik in April 1975, Sqn.Ldr. Inamdar was already there on deputation as a Test Pilot. He was a brilliant officer, with enormous energy and enthusiasm, and a delightfully cheerful demeanour. Since I was new to test flying of the MiG-21, he was a great help in guiding me into the game. He went back to the IAF mainstream, and in due course, rose to the rank of Air Marshal and retired as Vice Chief of Air Staff.

Soon, Flt.Lt. Rakesh (Ricky) Sharma came on deputation as a Test Pilot. This was prior to his selection to go into space as an astronaut, along with Russian astronauts in USSR, and to gain the status of a celebrity. He was an exceptional officer with a high sense of values, and impeccable integrity. We had a joyous bonding during our stay together at HAL Nasik, where we did a lot of flying together, and interacted on many technical issues. After his stint as an astronaut in USSR, he got back into the IAF, but soon enough, came back as a Test Pilot to HAL on a permanent basis.

Soon after, Sqn. Ldr. Viju Joshi also came on deputation as a Test Pilot. He was a keen and thorough test pilot and a good member of our team. He was quite a unique character, with some unusual talents. He was very good with his hands, and would often be seen with pieces of plywood and a pen-knife on his table, carving out aeroplane parts with great finesse, and assembling them with gum to make beautiful aircraft models. It would be perfectly to scale, with all details taken care of – quite an amazing effort. He also played the violin fairly well and would do so on occasions.

Towards the end of my tenure at HAL Nasik, two other test pilots came on deputation – Sqn. Ldr. Rajesh Lal and Sqn.Ldr. Vasudev. Both were gentle, friendly personalities, and performed their tasks with keenness and dedication. After completing their tenure at HAL, both got back to the IAF. While Rajesh rose to Air rank before retiring, Vasu left Airforce and moved to Air India and was pushing Boeing 747s across international routes.

Before leaving HAL, Vasu had a miraculous escape from a crash near the runway. He was returning from a test flight on the MiG 21 and was on final approach for landing, when he had a sudden loss of power. His aircraft sank and hit the ground a hundred yards or so short of the runway and rolled over a full 360°, both wings sheared off in the process, and the fuselage came to a stop with the cockpit right side up. I was also airborne at that time and approaching the airfield. I could see smoke bellowing from the crash, and the ATC asked me to standby for landing. I hoped the whole thing did not go up in flames. Soon, I was cleared to land, and as I hopped out of the aircraft, I was told that the pilot was safe, and had been shifted to the HAL hospital in the campus. I rushed to the hospital and saw him stretched out on a bed with a bandage on his hand. He gave me a big smile the moment he saw me.

When I asked him what happened, he narrated the event as follows: After crashing on to the ground, when the fuselage came to a halt after a 360 degree roll on the ground, he tried to jettison the canopy to escape, but it would not jettison (probably jammed due to distortion, as a result of the 360° roll on the ground). Anyway, he saw that the canopy had broken up at one point, and he managed to somehow squeeze out through the gap. There was a small temporary fire which caused him burns on the gloved hand, but he was otherwise in one piece. It was a miracle that the whole aircraft did not burst into flames. It was also a stroke of luck that the rolling of the aircraft after hitting the ground, caused the canopy to break, and for the fuselage to stop right side up, thus enabling the pilot to escape! Otherwise, he would have been well and truly trapped. No wonder, he gave me the sweetest smile he could muster when he saw me. It was a great relief to me that my young pilot was safe through such a major crash. We pilots have a belief that if your number is not up, you will always survive even the worst. Obviously, young Vasu's number was not up – God bless him!

For some years during my stay at HAL Nasik, the design department was headed by Kota Harinarayana (who later masterminded the design and development of the Light Combat Aircraft at Bangalore). He was an exceptional officer with a fantastic all-round knowledge of aerodynamics, flight mechanics, aircraft performance and systems; and an irrepressible enthusiasm to match. We hit it off really well right from the start. Both of us were deeply committed to improving the performance capabilities of the MiG 21. He had a very fertile mind, and came up with innovative ideas. A number of modifications were tried on the aircraft, and I looked forward to checking them out in the air. We worked together in an excellent supportive partnership. It was a great learning experience for me, and I still cherish happy memories of those fruitful days. Later, when I got transferred to HAL Bangalore, I again had the pleasure of working with Kota on the LCA project, which he so ably headed.

The HAL Township at Ojhar was quite unique. Spread over a large area, adjacent to the Bombay-Agra highway, it was 20km east of Nasik city. A large proportion of the work force – both officers and workers – stayed in the township. Numerous residential blocks housed the workers and junior staff, and the more senior officers were allotted independent villa-like houses with large compounds. There was a shopping centre in the middle of the campus with a movie theatre adjacent to it, as well as a high school and a hospital. Neat tar roads ran across the campus, flanked by rows of small trees. The soil there was jet black in colour and did not easily disintegrate into dust. The air was thus clean, and the sky a clear blue most months. The fresh air and long clean roads were most inviting for a walk or a jog. I would regularly go for a brisk walk and jog before sunrise, and then end up doing deep breathing, watching the sun pop up over the vineyards to the east. It did wonders to my mental state; especially with the happy thought that a few silver beauties would be waiting to spread their wings when I reported for work!

Management Experience

In the year 1980, the HAL high command decided to give management experience to some older test pilots of the company, so as to enable them to be usefully employed if they decided to quit flying for any reason. As a result, I was appointed as Deputy General Manager (DGM-O) for the Overhaul Division. I was not overly keen to get into the management stream, as I hoped to continue flying until my retirement at the age of 58 years. However, I did not mind having a bash at technical management as it would be a novel experience for a Test Pilot. I was, of course, to continue as Chief Test Pilot also, thus wearing two hats!

On one occasion, the personnel department was having an unpleasant confrontation with the labour union. They were deadlocked over some long pending issues. The Chief Administrative Manager sought a meeting with me along with the union leaders, to try and find a solution. When I heard them over, I realized that some of their demands were quite legitimate, but they also raised other points which were not reasonable, and not in the long term interests of the company. I told the union leader that I would fully support some of their demands, but they too must understand the views of the management and not make demands which are not in the interest of the company. That the company's health must matter to them also, as it was their own company. This seemed to soften them up and they agreed to cooperate. The deadlock was thus broken. The Admin Manager promptly reported to the General Manager, " Sir, hats off to Wg.Cdr. Ashoka for defusing the situation!" This was my first brush with the belligerent union, and I was happy with the result.

After about a year in my new assignment, the management introduced an incentive scheme for the workers. Each and every task at the worker level was studied by an expert team to assess how many hours would be needed to complete the task with reasonable efficiency and good effort. The component produced must, of course, meet the quality standards laid down. If the worker could complete the task in less than the stipulated time, he would get a bonus payment; and the faster he could complete the task, the greater would be the bonus. Initially, the workers went slow with the work, so that they could prove that the hours allotted were too stringent and could demand an increase in allotted time. This would enable them to earn a bigger bonus with less effort, but was not really in the interest of better productivity. On the other hand, if the hours allotted were too rigid, a good bonus would be out of their reach, and hence would not provide the incentive that we wished to provide. A reasonable balance had to be struck, where the incentive bonus was within reach, but with some concerted effort and better efficiency. It took many months of trial and adjustment, to reach the optimum allotted hours. But once it was settled and agreed upon, the productivity shot up remarkably, and the workers got a good bonus. By the second year after I took over, the whole division worked with great motivation and efficiency, and we overhauled a record 100 plus aircraft in one year! The HAL corporate office even quoted the Overhaul Division at HAL Nasik as an example to emulate.

By April 1983, I got my orders to move to HAL Bangalore as Chief Test Pilot there. That brought to an end a most challenging and rewarding eight years at HAL Nasik. It was a wrench to bid farewell to the MiG 21, though not for good. I would still return to Ojhar from Bangalore as often as possible, to jump into the MiG 21 cockpit and blaze away into the deep blue sky! Something I continued to do till my retirement from HAL in Oct.1992.

Author as Pilot Officer 1954

No.1 Vampire Squadron Jamnagar 1954

No.1 Vampire Squadron Palam 1954

Author in Vampire

In the Gnat Apr. 1960

22nd Course ETPS 1963 - Author 4th from Left, First Row Standing

Receiving Hawker Hunter
Trophy ETPS 3 December 1963
Farnborough, UK

Scimitar

VC-10

Auster 9

Otter

Toofani

Ilyushin 14

HF24 Marut

Tiger Moth

Harvard

Vampire

HT 2

Mystere IV

Gnat

Dc-3 Dakota

Chipmunk

Metor8   Hunter

Piston Provost

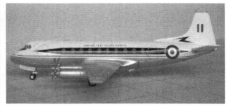

Devon   Viscount

Ashoka in MiG 21 Cockpit

Avro over Ganges

Barely missing a gruesome collision on take off at Kumbhigram (Sketch by Arun Swaminathan)

Receiving Vayu Sena Medal from AM Arjun Singh 1969

MiG 21 after last flight Oct. 1992

MiG 27 ML

Author with Jaguar

With HAL Flight Test Group 2

With HAL Flight Test Group 1

Briefing by Dr. R. Damania Before Rutan Long EZ First Flight

After Microlight Flight with Wife

Preparing for first flight Hansa

Ashoka with Hansa at Hyderabad

Author with Son & Family

Receiving Memento from ASTE

With Hansa 28 Nov. 2002

Hindustan Aeronautics Ltd Bangalore
Part I

Light Aircraft, Jet Trainers, Fighters & Bombers

I arrived in Bangalore in April 1983 to take over as Chief Test Pilot (CTP) at HAL Bangalore Complex. By then, I had been promoted to the rank of Additional General Manager, and was allotted a bungalow at the colony earmarked for senior officers. The colony, situated on Old Madras Road, was then called Bristol Quarters, as it was originally built to accommodate British Engineers belonging to Bristol Siddley Company, which had designed the Orpheus engine for the Gnat. HAL's engine factory, which was located close by, was producing this engine under license. The name, Bristol Quarters, was later changed to Senior Officer's Enclave. It was a gated colony with large bungalows surrounded by tall rain trees and abundant space for a garden. I had the pleasure of living in the colony for almost a decade, till I retired in 1992.

The CTP's office was located on the first floor of the Flight Test building, which accommodated all the Test Pilots and Flight Test engineers, as well as the office staff. My office had large windows overlooking the runway, with Bellandur Lake beyond. Sitting in my office, I could watch all aircraft movements on the runway. At that time, the CTP was also in-charge of the airfield and its administration, with the Aerodrome Officer working under him.

We had a good spread of aircraft types that came up for flight tests: the piston engine trainer aircraft HT2 and HPT32, the turboprop trainer HTT-34, the basic jet trainers Kiran MKI and Kiran MKII, the transonic fighters Ajeet and Ajeet Trainer, the supersonic ground attack fighter Jaguar, Canberra jet bombers in various versions, the C-119 Packet transport aircraft, and an occasional Devon commuter aircraft. And in Helicopters, the French Alouette and Cheetah. All these machines in one plate made for quite a sumptuous dish, and I had a keen appetite!

On my team was Sqn. Ldr 'Suzie' Apte, a very intelligent and jovial officer and a superb flyer. His contributions to test flying were significant. He had a great sense of humour, and his presence in a group could always be confirmed by the peels of laughter emanating from there. There was also a child-like quality to his personality, which was very endearing. After leaving HAL, he took to flying commuter aircraft for corporates. With him was Sqn. Ldr. PK Tayal (PKT), a hard working and methodical test pilot, who was sincere and well disciplined. To fly the Chairman's HS-748 aircraft, we got Wg.Cdr. Metrani. I had known him a little from earlier times. Matty, as we called him, was a very able pilot and a likeable human being, and I always enjoyed his company, inside as well as outside the Avro cockpit.

Some years down the line, two new fixed wing test pilots joined HAL on a permanent basis: Ashok Yadav and Baldev Singh, both Sqn. Ldrs. from the IAF. Baldev Singh (or Baldy, as he was called) was just starting his test flying career with HAL, while Ashok Yadav was more senior. Baldev was an excellent pilot- very sincere and methodical in all he did, and eventually became the Chief Test Pilot of HAL Bangalore and Executive Director.

In due course, I came to know Ashok Yadav well as we did a lot of flying together, particularly on the Ajeet trainer. He was a keen flyer and we would often discuss test flying matters late into the evening after I came back from a Jaguar sortie, close to sunset. He would always make it a point to stay back till I landed.

Light Aircraft

HT2, HPT32 and HTT34

The HT-2 was an all-metal piston engine basic trainer aircraft which was designed and built in HAL Bangalore. It had served the IAF for a very long time and was now nearing the end of its life. But a relatively small number still came to HAL for overhaul. It was a tail wheel aircraft, requiring just that much greater attention during takeoff and landing. It had conventional manual flight controls and a trim tab for the elevator. The controls were well harmonized and pleasant on feel. It had two cockpits, one behind the other, and had the classic characteristics of a basic trainer. Though quite underpowered, it was still a fully aerobatic machine, and of course, cleared for spinning. After flying high speed jet fighters, it was a refreshing change to fly this aircraft whenever it came up. It was nice to have only a handful of checks to do before takeoff – against some 100 odd actions on the Jaguar!

The HPT-32 was also a single piston engine basic trainer, but of a more advanced design, which was under development to replace the HT-2. The IAF had ordered a fairly large number of these aircraft. Once the development flight tests were over, the aircraft was to be manufactured at HAL, Kanpur. I was able to get some flying on the aircraft towards the end of its development flight testing. It was a nose wheel aircraft with side by side seating. A nose wheel aircraft is relatively easier to handle during takeoff and landing, and is less prone to bumps on landing or to yawing off on the landing run. The reason for this lies in the position of the centre of gravity (C.G.) in relation to the main wheels. In a nose wheel aircraft, the C.G. is ahead of the main wheels, while in a tail wheel aircraft, it is behind the main wheels. Thus, if the latter aircraft lands with a thump on its main wheels, the tail is pushed down due to inertia effect, which causes the nose to pitch UP. This results in an increase in the angle of attack of the wings, resulting in greater lift, which in turn makes the aircraft get airborne again. This results in a series of uncontrolled bumps, hiking up the pilot's blood pressure! On the nose wheel aircraft, on the other hand, a hard landing causes the nose to come *down*, and the aircraft attains a stable 3 point attitude, without causing any further bumps. In a similar way, if the tail wheel aircraft experiences an unwanted yaw on the landing run, the inertia effect of the c.g would aggravate the yaw, while on a nose wheel aircraft, it would dampen it. The ground loop during the landing run is a speciality only of a tail wheel aircraft. The HPT-32 was thus, much easier on the trainee pilot, who is anyway straining to make a safe landing.

Acceptance of the HPT-32 by the IAF was held up for some years, because some of their test pilots thought it's spinning characteristics were unacceptable, while HAL's Test Pilots found it acceptable. It became a contentious issue between HAL and the IAF, and a group of very senior IAF officers was appointed to check its acceptability. After numerous test flights, their unanimous decision was that though it's spinning characteristics were not exactly what was stipulated in the Air Staff Requirements (ASR), it was nevertheless, acceptable for its role. This event highlighted the need for test pilots to be willing to compromise a little on matters which are not of a critical nature. I have come to realise that an aircraft's performance is invariably a product of some compromise – you just cannot have all you want. A broad pragmatic view, with a sense of proportion, is essential to ensure that progress of a project does not get jeopardized in the impracticable pursuit of perfection.

At a later stage, HAL had modified one HPT-32 airframe, and fitted a much more powerful turbo-prop engine to it – naming the new machine HTT-34 (for Hindustan Turbo Trainer-34). The aim was to enhance its performance, while also overcoming the nagging supply problems of high octane fuel. The turbo-prop engine, of course, uses turbine fuel (like refined kerosene), which is available plentifully. The more powerful turbine engine on the HTT-34 gave the aircraft excellent aerobatic capability, and remarkable all round performance. We demonstrated the aircraft at Farnborough (UK) and Paris air shows in 1984 and 1985 respectively. Later, we took it to Nigeria and Ghana in Africa on a marketing mission. Our aerobatic displays were greatly appreciated and some of the foreign pilots who flew the aircraft, were also duly impressed. Unfortunately, this did not result in any sales – probably for financial reasons. So, a beautiful aircraft had to be assigned to posterity! Sadly, this happens quite often in the aviation world, competition being what it is.

On 28th March 1988, I was called by my Chairman, Air Marshal Wollen, and told that some seven HPT-32 aircraft at HAL Kanpur were not being cleared by the test pilots there, as they found the stall behaviour unacceptable. There was reportedly an excessive wing drop at stall – a phenomenon caused by one wing stalling a little before the other. The IAF had stipulated that any wing drop at stall beyond 20 deg. bank, would not be accepted.

So, I was asked to proceed forthwith to Kanpur to try and solve the problem. The deadline for clearing all the aircraft planned for the financial year was 31st March. If the target was not met by that date, there were some serious financial implications, in addition to loss of face for the company. Since it was already 28th March, there was no time to lose. In view of the urgency, I was authorised to take the Chairman's Avro to Kanpur. I took off along with Metrani, the same evening, and landed at Kanpur close to midnight.

The next day, I talked to the pilots there, and they confirmed that since they had experienced a wing drop greater than 20 deg. at stall, they could not clear the aircraft. I decided to fly a few aircraft to check on the problem. On the first aircraft, when I carried out a stall, I found that there was only a mild wing drop of just 5 deg. or so – it was a perfectly docile stall, and totally acceptable. I was surprised at the happy result and went ahead and carried out the spinning test, which was kept pending, and found that too perfectly normal. I landed back and cleared the aircraft and asked the ground staff to offer all the remaining aircraft also for flight. I flew all the remaining six aircraft one by one, and found all of them behaving normally; in fact, they did not have any wing drop at all! I completed the spinning tests on all the aircraft, and cleared them. After a midnight landing in the Avro the previous night, carrying out 8 flights the next day, left me totally fatigued. But the joy of completing the task successfully was compensation enough. It was a mystery why the pilots there did not clear the aircraft. I presume it was some management issue, which they would settle in due course.

Jet Trainers

Kiran MK 1

The Kiran MK I was the first basic jet trainer designed and built by HAL Bangalore in the late sixties. It had two side by side seats, and was used extensively over many decades by the IAF for basic jet aircraft training. When I came to HAL Bangalore, this aircraft was being overhauled there, so I got to do quite a lot of flying on it. It was a sweet machine, and had just the right mix of complexity and performance to initiate a young pilot into jet aircraft flying. It was, of course, a nose wheel aircraft, and had normal manual flight controls, which were very pleasant and well harmonized. It was pressurized and fully aerobatic. What is more, it had excellent stall and spin characteristics.

Kiran Mk 2

Later, the HAL designers brought out a MK 2 version of the Kiran, with a more powerful Orpheus engine of Gnat fame. This engine had to be de-rated to suit the Kiran. The aircraft was also provided with limited weapons capability for advanced training. The Kiran MK 2 was in production when I came to HAL Bangalore, and I did a lot of production flight tests on it.

Though the MK 2 was not significantly different in shape and size to MK I, its flying qualities were quite a bit different in some respects. Generally, it was not as smooth and pleasant to fly as MK I, in spite of better acceleration and climb capability due to the more powerful engine. Also, its spin characteristics were much different, being more oscillatory and at times, even violent. However, if the spins were restricted to 2 or 3 turns, its behaviour was acceptable.

Another peculiarity of the Kiran MK2 was the tendency of the ailerons to get "over-balanced" temporarily after spinning was carried out. Most manual control aircraft have their control surfaces aerodynamically "balanced" by design .This reduces the pilot force required to move it against air resistance. If, for some reason, the balancing effect becomes excessive, an overbalance results, causing the control surface to move off to a higher angle than what the pilot desires. This results in severe deterioration in pilot's control feel, and hence in the ease of flying. On the Kiran MK 2, aileron balancing was achieved by shaping the aileron leading(i.e. front) edge, in a specific fashion. It occurred to me that since this overbalance problem was occurring as a temporary phenomenon only after spinning, the ailerons were probably taking a somewhat different position after a few spins. Since a spin results in sustained very high angles of attack, the ailerons were probably being forced up a bit (the control linkages can get stretched to permit this). This would alter the airflow pattern at the leading edge of the aileron, creating this phenomenon. For achieving the right level of balancing of flight controls, the angle at which they are rigged is a critical factor. Any deviation in this can upset the level of balancing. On my recommendation, both ailerons were rigged down by 1 deg to compensate for the possible up- float; and the problem was solved. Of course, the aileron control force did increase a bit, but it was acceptable(You just cannot have everything you want!). Avoiding control overbalance is one of the critical points during initial flight testing of prototype aircraft with manual controls. But sometimes, a degree of over-balance has to be accepted under concession, if it does not otherwise corrupt the control feel of the pilot as a whole. Here, it was spoiling the control feel significantly, and I was glad that we were able to solve the problem.

While Kiran MK 2 had nearly completed its developmental flight tests, there was one test which had been pending for long, and had yet to be carried out. This was to demonstrate a safe recovery from an *inverted* spin. HAL test pilots had earlier taken a stand that the aircraft was totally resistant to getting into an inverted spin, and hence the test cannot be carried out. But the IAF was adamant that the aircraft could not be inducted into service, unless this test was done and a safe recovery demonstrated. The whole responsibility now fell on my shoulders, and I felt that it was our duty to do our best and somehow complete this test, and obtain a final clearance for the aircraft. Much was at stake, and the prolonged deadlock on the issue needed to be broken .

Inverted spin is a tricky manoeuvre, and successful recovery cannot always be guaranteed. What is more, the aircraft did not have an anti-spin parachute, which is an essential safety device to facilitate recovery in case the aircraft does not recover with normal procedure. However, it is a rather long drawn process to have an anti-spin parachute installed and tested for reliable deployment. This should have been done earlier, but for some reason, it had been kept in abeyance, possibly in the hope that such a test may not be necessary. Anyway, in view of the pressing need to obtain full clearance of the aircraft at the earliest, I decided to go ahead without the anti-spin chute. It was a risk I was taking, but I had the confidence that I would be able to tackle it. As I was told that earlier standard attempts to enter inverted spin had not proved successful, I thought it necessary to think of some other novel method. I knew that the aircraft was most vulnerable at the point when it stops rotating during recovery from a normal erect spin. At this point, when you are in a steep dive, but at a very low speed, pushing the stick fully forward abruptly, and applying full rudder may do the trick, and get us into an inverted spin!

So, one fine morning, I got airborne along with Ashok Yadav, to push the aircraft as best as possible into an inverted spin, hoping to recover safely. We climbed to 20,000 ft and first carried out a normal two turn erect spin and recovered. After that we climbed up again to 25,000 ft, and this time, I decided to push her into an inverted spin. So, we got into a normal spin, and the moment the rotation ceased during recovery, I banged the stick fully forward and applied full left rudder. Nothing happened for a brief moment, but I kept the stick fully forward for another second or so, and the aircraft flicked into an inverted spin. I held the in-spin controls and found that it was a smooth ride – almost an anti-climax! (The normal *erect* spin was much more oscillatory). After 2-3 turns, I centralised the rudder and brought the stick *back* towards the neutral position, and the spin stopped immediately. Hurrah! We had done it. I pulled the aircraft out of the steep dive and put her into a climb, and breathed a sigh of relief!

I then handed over the controls to Ashok Yadav and asked him to have a go at it. He climbed back to 25,000 ft and went through the process, but the aircraft refused to enter into an inverted spin. After he pulled out of the dive, I asked him to try once more. He tried again but the aircraft just would not go into an inverted spin! I said I would try one more time and then we would return to base. On this second attempt also, I was able to repeat the inverted spin, and recovered safely. Obviously, the aircraft had a soft corner for me! Anyway, I was really pleased that we had managed to complete this long pending test successfully .

Next morning, the flight test engineers showed the recorded results, and one could see the typical inverted spin features. In a normal spin, the yawing and rolling are to the same side in relation to the aircraft axes, but in an inverted spin they are to opposite sides. This was clearly seen in the in-flight recorder traces. ASTE flight engineers also examined the results and were fully satisfied with them. Everyone was surprised that I had managed to carry out this long pending test successfully - and that too without an anti-spin chute! As they say, where there is a will, there is always a way, and if your approach is right, Providence will always back you up.

Jet Fighters

Ajeet

The Ajeet was a modified Gnat MK I, with greater fuel capacity and better weapons capability. It also had a ground level ejection seat, the lack of which on Gnat MK I had caused numerous fatalities. The engine remained the Orpheus, as in Gnat MK 1. But since the weight of the aircraft had increased, its performance had deteriorated somewhat, making it more sober and gentlemanly. It could not quite give the sort of kick that came so naturally from the Gnat. Its handling characteristics, however, remained more or less the same.

Ajeet Trainer

HAL designers developed a two seat version of the Ajeet – the Ajeet Trainer – with two cockpits in tandem (that is, one behind the other), and all the controls duplicated. The aircraft fuselage had to be lengthened quite a bit to accommodate the two cockpits. Other than that, there was no significant change in its shape.

Before I came to Bangalore in early 1983, a fatal accident had occurred on the first prototype. The next prototype came up only in March 1984, and Sqn.Ldr. Tayal and I carried out the first flight of the aircraft. Because of the fatal accident, there was an air of apprehension regarding the Ajeet Trainer, though the investigation into the accident had concluded the cause of the accident to be mismanagement of the oxygen system by the pilot. I could sense a somewhat overcautious approach prevailing towards the aircraft. I decided that we had to break the ice, and get on to vigorous test flying to prove the aircraft. After doing a few dual flights to familiarize myself, I took the aircraft by myself and carried out some intense aerobatics, just to feel more comfortable. I found the aircraft to be a bit sluggish compared to the single seat Ajeet, but otherwise, quite nice to handle.

Soon, Sqn. Ldr. Tayal was transferred to HAL Kanpur, and Sqn. Ldr. Ashok Yadav got onto the project with me. I decided to push the flight test programme on the Ajeet Trainer, so as to complete all the development flying by the fast approaching deadline. There was quite a bit of testing left to be done; performance measurements, night flying, armament trials, engine relights in the air, and finally spinning. Normally, it was the practice then, to carry out only one development flight per day, so that there was enough time to analyse all the results and carry out any required changes before the next flight. But, in view of the urgency to meet the deadline, we decided to carry out two flights a day. We did performance tests in the mornings and handling tests in the afternoon. Since the results of the performance tests were not relevant to the handling tests in the next flight, this arrangement worked very well and we were able to speed up the work.

I deputed Sqn. Ldr.Yadav to fly the aircraft out to Kalaikunda and carryout the armament trials. This he did pretty quickly with satisfactory results. We then took up night flying trials at Bangalore, and carried out a number of flights on dark nights, checking among other things, the ease of landing from the rear cockpit without using landing lights! The forward view from the rear cockpit was much worse compared to the front cockpit, but I got the hang of it with a little practice. I carried out many touch and go landings from the rear cockpit and felt quite comfortable. The pupil would, of course, fly from the front cockpit, which provided a grand forward view, just like the single seat Ajeet.

The next test was to check restarting the engine in the air. For this, of course, we needed to first switch off the engine. We decided to first carryout a simulated forced landing on the runway with, engine throttled back to idle power, to get a feel of the descent rate, and to refine our judgement. This would facilitate a successful forced landing, in case we could not restart the engine in the air. After this was done, we climbed back to 20,000ft, switched off the engine, and carried out relights at the stipulated speeds. We found the relights to be successful every time.

Then came the critical spin trials, the last bit of flight testing on the Ajeet Trainer, before it could be cleared for delivery to IAF. Having once ejected from the Gnat in a "never-ending" spin, I was naturally a bit apprehensive, and was mentally prepared for another ejection, if that was the way things turned out. Of course, being a prototype, we had the benefit of an anti-spin tail chute, which was fitted on the aircraft. If the aircraft could not be recovered through stipulated flight control inputs, the chute would be deployed. This would cause the yawing motion to be drastically reduced, and possibly, pitch the aircraft nose down, thus facilitating recovery.

I went up with Ashok Yadav in the rear cockpit, to carry out the first spins, hoping that it would recover. We climbed to 30,000 ft and levelled out. I throttled the engine all the way to idle RPM, and progressively got the stick back to reduce the speed gradually and approach the stall. As we neared the stall, there was an increase in buffet, and I applied full left rudder and pulled the stick fully back. The aircraft nose went up a bit, then sliced to the left and dropped well below the horizon. Surprisingly, the ensuing rolling motion was quite moderate, but the slicing (yawing) was severe, and continued with interruptions. Altogether, it was not a vigorous spin, though the off and on yawing threw the pilot's body sideways to cause some discomfort. After 2-3 turns, I applied the recommended recovery controls – (opposite rudder and stick forward), and the aircraft recovered gradually in steps, as if reluctant to do so. The yawing to left and right ebbed away gradually, and finally ceased completely, with the aircraft in a steep dive. I pulled her out of the dive by 15,000 ft or so. Thereafter, we climbed up and carried out one spin to the other side and recovered satisfactorily. After that, we headed back to base and landed.

The whole test was recorded onboard, to be analysed later. Next morning, the results of the analysis were available and we got a go-ahead for carrying out some more spins to check repeatability. Ashok Yadav and I carried out a few more flights, alternately piloting the aircraft and doing the spins. The behaviour of the aircraft during the spins and recovery was dramatically different from what I had experienced on the single seat Gnat. The spin is known to be very sensitive to small aerodynamic changes. And in this case, the change was profound, as the length of aircraft had been increased quite substantially. I am sure this made a big favourable difference in recovery .

Once our tests were over, I took up some test pilots from ASTE, IAF, to demonstrate to them the aircraft behaviour in spin and all were well pleased with the aircraft's behaviour. Thus ended our development flights on the Ajeet Trainer. We had cleared the aircraft well before the deadline, to the gleeful surprise of HAL management, who were often faced with time over- runs.

One day, on a general handling and aerobatic sortie on the Ajeet Trainer, I was faced with a serious control problem. I was checking out what 'g' the aircraft could sustain in a tight turn at 10,000 ft at a speed of 400 knots. I increased the 'g' progressively, reaching 7g. But when I wanted to come out of the turn, I found that my stick was jammed, and I could not recover from the turn. It was a dangerous position to get struck in, as I could easily black out if the high g condition persisted. I could not think of anything else but to split the tail. As I pulled back the lever, the control column (stick) jerked and became free, and I regained full control. On the Gnat,(as well as on the Ajeet and Ajeet trainer), there was a provision to *split* the tail plane, whereby a small portion of the elevator detaches itself from the hydraulically powered tail plane, and could be moved manually by the pilot. This was meant primarily to cater to a hydraulic failure, which would render the large front portion of the hydraulically powered tail plane immovable. Splitting the tail, thus, provided some minimum pitch control to land the aircraft safely. In this instance, of course, there was no hydraulic failure, and so once the stick became free, I regained full control. However, I had to exercise caution to ensure that the jamming did not occur again, particularly during landing. I kept a low speed and used elevator very gently to return to base, and landed safely.

When the technical personnel checked the elevator circuit, they found evidence of a mechanical restriction of the control cable at one spot, where it passes through a cut- out in the structure. This meant that I was plain lucky that it did not happen again before I landed! Anyway, a suitable modification was done to overcome the problem. It was a somewhat scary experience, and entirely on account of insufficient attention during detailed design stage. An easily avoidable situation.

xxxxx

Test flying regularly day after day does get a bit tiring. So, I loved to fly the Chairman's Avro aircraft whenever possible. Often, when the chairman had to visit Delhi for some meeting or the other, it would involve a late night 5-hour return flight. A long night flight in the cockpit of a transport aircraft is quite a unique experience. For one, the atmosphere is cool, and provides a smooth ride - and the aircraft just loves it. The cockpit is pretty dark, except for some indirect lighting and the gentle glow of the instruments. The engines are synchronized to a steady drone, and the autopilot keeps the aircraft on course and on an even keel. The radio is also mostly silent at night, and one can feel the unusual sense of peace pervading the cockpit – so unlike a fighter cockpit, where the intensity of tasks at hand keeps the pilot on edge. With the Chairman on board, there would also be a regular supply of goodies in flight –chips, cashew nuts ,sandwiches and pastries, and of course some hot coffee -which the steward would bring up to the cockpit from time to time throughout the flight ,and we would thoroughly enjoy a coffee break!

On a clear night, the various cities en-route would glow with a thousand lights visible from a 100 miles. And at times, while flying over a sparklingly lit-up city, a diaphanous sheet of thin cloud would sneak over it, transforming it into an ethereal treasure trove of jewels. What amazing beauty a mere wisp of a cloud can create!

Jaguar

When I moved to HAL Bangalore in April 1983, the two -engine Jaguar Strike Fighter aircraft had just been inducted into IAF service in fly-away condition. I had not flown the Jaguar earlier, so I took a few familiarization flights on the 2-seater with Sqn.Ldr. Ajit Agtey, a senior Test Pilot from ASTE, and then went up on my own. Thereafter, the first single seat Jaguar came up for test flights in August 1983, and I carried out the full flight test schedule on this single seat version. After clearing the schedule, I did several more flights just to familiarize with this new beauty of a fighter.

The Jaguar had numerous novel features, incorporating a number of the latest technologies in aviation. Its airframe was optimized for low level strike role. Since this implied flying at very low altitudes at high speeds, and often in turbulent conditions, special care was taken in the design to minimise the effect of turbulence, the prolonged exposure to which could cause severe fatigue to the pilot. This was achieved by having a relatively small wing area for the weight of the aircraft, thus giving what is called a higher 'wing loading'. Just as, on rough seas, a heavily loaded boat would not get thrown around as much as an empty one, similarly an aircraft with high wing loading would give a much smoother ride through turbulence. However, smaller wings impose a penalty in terms of the total lift they can generate. Thus, the turning performance of the Jaguar had to be compromised to a degree, since tight turns require high lift capability. As a result, while the aircraft was superb in the low-level strike role, it was not an aircraft for sustained dog fight, where good turning performance is crucial. But then, aircraft design is always a compromise based on priorities – If you want one thing, you have to be ready to give up on something else!

Another significant aspect of its design pertained to its engines. These jet engines, named Adour, incorporated what is known as the 'bypass principle'. This lowers the fuel consumption and enhances the aircraft's range and endurance. This is done by not allowing all the compressed air from the compressor assembly, to go through the combustion cycle. Some of it was made to bypass the combustion chamber, and directed to mix with the hot gases emerging at the exhaust. This results in reducing the mean velocity and temperature of the exhaust gases as a whole, thus minimizing waste of energy. This in turn results in better engine efficiency, which means lower fuel consumption for a given engine thrust. The Jaguar was one of the earliest fighter aircraft to have such 'bypass' engines, and indeed the very first one in the IAF.

The Adour engine also had an afterburner system to give it added thrust to enhance takeoff performance, as well as to give better acceleration to get away safely after hitting the target. While, at low altitudes, the after burner operated quite well, its operation at higher altitudes was not that reliable.

We had one test in the flight test schedule, where we had to carry out a climb to 40,000 ft with both engines in full after-burner to check engine stability at high altitudes. On occasions, the engine would flame out with a bang, and would have to be re-started in the air. I think the reason for poor afterburner stability at high altitude was the lower pressure in the exhaust due to the bypass. Anyway, the aircraft was not designed to operate at high altitudes in afterburner mode, so it was an acceptable compromise.

We also had a test point to go supersonic at high altitude and then dive to lower levels and reach a speed of 750 Knots. It was a struggle to go beyond 1.3 Mach, but it handled very well right up to 750 Knots at a low level.

In order to enable a long-range strike aircraft to attack targets relatively deep inside enemy territory with precision, it needs a good navigation and attack (Nav-attack) system. For the first time in the IAF, we had in Jaguar, an Inertial Nav-attack system to fulfil this requirement effectively. This is a "gyro and accelerometer" based computerized system which can provide accurate navigation and precise attack capability. It is totally self-contained and hence cannot be jammed by the enemy. It was quite a sophisticated system, but extremely pilot friendly. Before undertaking a flight, its gyro-stabilized Inertial platform is first aligned with the North direction. Then the exact position of the aircraft as well as the target in terms of Latitude and Longitude, is fed into the computer. Now, when the aircraft starts taxiing out for a flight, the sensitive accelerometers detect its motion in all directions, which the computer integrates into velocity (i.e. speed and direction). Since the starting point is known, and all subsequent movements are also sensed, the computer is able to integrate and analyse the information to provide continuous data about its current position. The standard for clearing the aircraft, required an error of no more than one mile after flying for an hour, covering around 450 nautical miles.

What is more, the system had a provision for updating the aircraft position by flying over a known landmark and pressing the update button. This would nullify all accumulated errors, and bring the entire system to 100% accuracy. An update like this would necessarily be done just prior to going in for an attack, to enhance weapon delivery accuracy. In this system, when you approach the target, a synthetic target marker (like a cross) appears on the wind shield, indicating the exact position of the target. Thus, it was possible to release the weapons (bombs or rockets) without even sighting the target – most helpful in war-time blackout conditions on a dark night. As part of the Nav-attack system, an additional aid was provided by way of a moving- map display on a screen. This was a colour representation of the map of the area surrounding the flight path, with the aircraft position indicated on it. Thus, the pilot not only did not need to carry a map on his lap, but he did not even need to look out to check his position in the countryside.

In addition to all this, for the first time in the IAF, we had an aircraft with a Head Up Display or HUD, for short. This is an optical system which projects all essential flight and attitude information on to the windscreen directly in front of the pilot. The pilot, thus, does not need to look down to the instrument panel to check any of the flight parameters. It is a great boon to the pilot who is flying at high speed at a very low altitude, and needs all his attention to focus on the view straight ahead.

The Jaguar also had one of the best rocket-assisted ejection seats from the famous British firm – Martin Baker. This was what is called a 'zero-zero' ejection seat, meaning one could eject safely even at ground level at zero speed. The earlier ground level ejection seats required a minimum speed of 90 knots (such as during take-off), to eject safely. Zero-Zero ejection seat, of course, provides the ultimate safety to the pilot, as the following incident demonstrates: On one occasion (not in India), a Jaguar pilot who had just landed, found that one of his engines had caught fire on the landing run. By the time he brought the aircraft to a stop, thick flames had engulfed the entire aircraft, and naturally, he could not get out of the cockpit. He simply pulled the ejection handle, and found himself rocketed upwards, well clear of the flames, and high enough for the seat to separate, and the parachute to deploy fully before he touched down safely nearby. A really close shave! A superb escape system like this, along with its two engines, and an excellent Nav-attack system, makes the pilot feel really safe while flying the Jaguar. A great tribute to its designers. Thank you, Sirs!

We had one set navigation exercise to check out the accuracy of the Nav-attack system. This involved flying at low level at a speed of 450 Knots from Bangalore to Hosur, Krishnagiri, Mettur, and back to Hosur. Mock attacks were carried out at Krishnagiri and Mettur, both of which had juicy dams as targets! The leg from Mettur to Hosur, passed through a beautiful valley, resplendent with multi coloured foliage. Whizzing past the picturesque landscape with an excellent outside view from a cool and comfortable cockpit, was a treat.

The IAF wanted to use the Jaguar for maritime operations, with the capability to attack enemy warships. This required installation of a special radar called Agave on the nose of the aircraft. Two Jaguars were modified with these radars and came up for flight tests. We had first to check if this modification affected the handling characteristics of the aircraft, in view of some changes in the shape of the aircraft nose. We found that the aircraft behaviour was not really affected. Thereafter, we had to check the operational capability of the radar in detection of ships, and following it up by mock attacks. For this, we would fly on to the sea past Chennai at low level, and use the radar to detect any ship sailing there, and then carry out mock attacks on it. We made similar flights westward on to the Arabian Sea beyond Mangalore, and carried out a few attacks on ships there as well. The system worked very well, and the trials were a great success. Flying a fighter aircraft low over the blue sea at high speed has its own charm. In due course, a number of Jaguars were fitted with this system, and the IAF formed a few Jaguar Squadrons for maritime operations.

I also found the Jaguar to be one of the most comfortable fighter aircraft I have flown. The cockpit was spacious, with excellent outside view. All cockpit controls were well designed and very smooth to operate. As the undercarriage legs were well articulated, with the wheels having low-pressure tyres, and smooth foot brakes and nose wheel steer, taxying the Jaguar gave the pilot the smoothest ride he could have on the ground. Because of this level of cushioning, it was also possible to get a truly silken landing on this aircraft. On one lucky day, I fluked a landing so smooth that I literally did not feel I had touched down. I had a similar experience on just one more occasion while landing the Piston Provost aircraft at ETPS, in U.K. Just two perfect landings in 50 years of flying. Nothing great, but I still get overjoyed when I think of the *perfection* of it.

Often, a Jaguar would be offered for test flight at HAL Bangalore late in the evening, close to pack-up time. I used to delight in taking up these flights, with the sun close to setting and the air cooling down to offer super aerodynamic smoothness! At the end of the tests, I would invariably carry out low-level aerobatics over the Bellandur Lake near the airfield, with the airspace entirely free of any other traffic. By the time I landed and taxied back to dispersal, the sun would have already set in flaming twilight colours. Ending the day with a late evening flight like this, the fatigue of the day's routine would vanish into thin air, leaving me with the warm glow of a day's work well done.

While carrying out low flying over the countryside in a Jaguar, I would often encounter a band of cattle or sheep, grazing lazily in quiet contentment. But the moment they hear the sound of an approaching aircraft, they would get scared and start running. One would expect them to run helter skelter, but surprisingly, they would do just the opposite; they would all converge towards a common central point, like the radii of a circle meeting at its centre. It was an exhibition of immaculate precision in geometry. I always wondered how they managed such precision, in perfect coordination, and that too so swiftly. Of course, they must be aiming for some kind of collective security, but executed with such utmost precision, and so spontaneously.

A similar, mysterious phenomenon can be noticed if you observe a large flock of, say, 20 or 30 birds, roaming the sky just for the fun of it. They would be flying in a close-knit formation, just inches apart from one another. All of a sudden, the whole formation would execute a sharp turn, still in perfect formation, with no hint of a possible collision. I know from my personal experience in formation flying on Fighters, that if the leader of a formation executes an abrupt turn without any warning, there would instantly be a massive collision. How the birds manage it so spontaneously is a real mystery. I have tried to understand such phenomena through the medium of physics, but to no avail. The answer possibly lies in the realm of *metaphysics*.

MiG 27

In July 1984, the first MiG 27 *swing wing* fighter had been assembled in HAL Nasik and flight tests had begun. Soon, I familiarised myself with the machine and thereafter flew it whenever I visited Nasik.

The MiG 27 was a ground attack fighter bomber with supersonic capability. It was a large and heavy aircraft as fighters go. It had a single powerful jet engine with afterburner, a good Nav Attack system and quite a formidable weapons capability. The real novelty was, of course, its swing wings, which could be positioned anywhere from 16 degrees to 72 degrees backward sweep.

There was a pivot point close to the wing root around which the wing could swivel. This was attained by operation of a lever on the left of the cockpit, close to throttle. The operation could be performed on the ground as well as in the air. The lever had three pre determined notches at 16, 45 and 72 degrees sweep. These were the recommended positions for three modes of flight: 16 degrees for slower speeds which included take-off, landing and cruise; 45 degrees was the position for air combat, weapon delivery and for most manoeuvres and aerobatics; and 72 degrees for supersonic flight and high-speed getaways after attacking the target. The handling qualities of these three wing positions were quite different, as also the limitations in terms of 'g', max speed and angle of attack.

Another noteworthy aspect of the design was that its lateral (i.e. rolling) control was through spoilers. These are flat surfaces which pop up over the wing to face the airflow, thus 'spoiling' or reducing the lift on that side and causing the wing to go down.

In the 72-degree wing sweep position, the spoilers were de-activated as they would not face the wind squarely and would thus lose their effectiveness. Lateral control was then achieved not through spoilers, but through differential movement of left and right parts of the horizontal tail plane.

The MiG 27 was quite a massive machine and not quite agile like the MiG 21. But its powerful engine enabled the pilot to attain rapid acceleration and even go supersonic. However, it was not quite suited for sustained dogfights.

One day, in 1990, we got news at Bangalore that a MiG 27 aircraft had crashed at Ojhar airfield at HAL Nasik, and that its pilot had been killed. I immediately flew down to Ojhar to check on what exactly happened. I was told that the pilot was carrying out low-level rolls on the aircraft, and the whole sequence was being filmed from the ground. We asked for the video to be screened, and it showed graphically the aircraft being rolled at low altitude with its wings at 72 deg. sweep position. It lost height while rolling out from the inverted position, and hit the runway and burst into flames.

What perplexed me was why the pilot had the wings at 72 deg. sweep – a wing position not meant for aerobatics at all. The pilots who were doing the filming described the exact sequence of events leading to the crash. He first carried out rolls over the runway at 45 deg. wing sweep position, the correct wing sweep for aerobatics, and all went well. Then, prior to the last run, he surprisingly, moved the wings to 72 deg. position and attempted a slow roll, during which the aircraft lost height and crashed.

It is my guess that since the whole sequence was being filmed, he wanted the aircraft to look as sleek as possible, and hence swept the wings to 72 deg. position. Apparently, he had not practiced a slow roll at 72 deg. wing position earlier at a safe height – something very fundamental – before attempting the same at low altitude. He appears to have done so on the spur of the moment, not realizing that rolling the aircraft at 72 deg. wing-sweep is altogether different from rolling it at 45 deg. sweep.

As mentioned earlier, at 72 degrees sweep, the system provides roll control through differential movement of the left and right parts of the tail plane. However, while doing so, the tail plane retains its primary function for pitch control. The total authority of the tail plane is, thus, shared between pitch and roll controls. Consequently, the authority of each stands diminished. This is particularly evident in manoeuvres where both these controls need to be used simultaneously in large doses – a classic case being a slow roll. In this manoeuvre, a large amount of pitch authority is used up while transiting through the inverted position, to keep the aircraft nose from dropping. As a result, not sufficient roll power is available for rolling the aircraft fast enough. In such a situation, if the aircraft is at a low altitude, and starts losing height while rolling out from the inverted position, as often happens, it could hit the ground before completing the roll. This is just what happened.

The crux of the matter, of course, is that what he attempted was unplanned and done on the spur of the moment, without first rehearsing it at a safe altitude, where loss of height would not have mattered. Indeed, he would have also realised that doing a slow roll in 72 deg. sweep position is not worth it, and unsafe at low altitude, as the safety margins are too narrow. I also feel that he may well have kept a lower speed as well for ease of filming, making matters worse.

While showmanship is part of a test pilot's job, it needs to be tempered with cool calculation and meticulous discipline. Letting wild impulses to overshadow the much needed care and caution, is only asking for trouble. Unfortunately, it is a trap pilots sometimes fall into, with grave consequences.

MiG 29

By early 1988, the Director of the LCA project had obtained approval for me to fly the MiG 29 fighter with the IAF. This was one of the best Air superiority fighters of the time acquired by the Air force. Since I was in the LCA team, it was felt that the project would benefit by my exposure to it.

In April of the same year, I landed up at IAF station Pune, where the first two MiG 29 squadrons were located. I went through the standard ground training, learning all about its systems, flying characteristics and so on. Then I got one dual sortie, and proceeded to do my solo.

The MiG 29 was a large aircraft with a maximum weight of 18 tons, and had two powerful after- burning jet engines in the fuselage, with a total thrust of 16,300 kg. The power- to- weight ratio of the aircraft was the best I had come across in a fighter. In a clean configuration, the thrust was higher than the weight. The aircraft was thus capable of demonstrating a vertical climb straight after getting airborne!

The aircraft had two large box- type air intakes for the two engines, located under the belly. Since these intakes were low-slung and close to the ground, there was a danger of sucking in small stones and other objects kicked up by the nose wheel during taxying, takeoff and landing. To prevent this, the air intakes were provided with large doors which would remain shut during ground operation. The engines would then suck air through auxiliary intakes provided on top of the wings. These would suffice for low-speed operation. However, once a speed of 200 kph was achieved during take-off, the large intake doors would open automatically, so that the engines could operate without constraint. But since the aircraft would still be on the take off run and accelerating, the pilot had to ensure that before this speed was reached, the nose wheel was lifted off the ground, so that loose objects kicked up by the nose wheel were not sucked in by the engine. Similarly, during landing, the nose wheel had to be held off the ground till the speed reduced below 200 Knots and the intake doors closed. It was a somewhat complicated procedure, but was easy to execute, and worked flawlessly.

The aircraft had all the necessary systems which high performance fighters must have:- an Inertial navigation system, a Head Up display for the pilot, a full fledged Auto pilot, and an Airborne Interception Radar which could detect targets at considerable range. For carriage of weapons, it had a total of six points – three under each wing, which could carry a variety of weapon loads. An additional large fuel tank could be carried under the belly. All in all, it could carry quite a considerable load for a fighter.

The aircraft had a unique facility called EKRAN to help the pilot monitor the health of various systems in flight. A small screen was provided on the instrument panel which would light up and display the item or system needing pilot's attention at that moment. An audio alert would command the pilot to look at the screen whenever a fresh display appeared. Thus, as long as the screen remained clear, all was well. With such a facility, the pilot did not need to monitor each and every system separately. This was an extremely pilot friendly feature – one quick glance at the screen to check it was clear, and you are done with complex monitoring. Such novel features in the design of the aircraft, made an otherwise pretty complex high-performance aircraft, appear to be a simple machine. A factor which enhances pilot confidence and a sense of safety in the aircraft. Typical Russian designers' horse sense.

From the very first flight, I found the aircraft very easy to handle throughout its flight envelope. Though the flight controls were only hydraulically powered and not fly-by-wire, the ease of handling was superb, and one hardly missed the delicacies of a fly-by-wire control! The two large engines provided an abundance of power, giving superb acceleration and climb performance. In fact, the standard operating procedure was to execute take off in dry power (i.e. without after burner). The aircraft got airborne at a speed of 250 Kmph, whereas even the lighter MiG 21 got airborne only around 300 kmph. On one takeoff, I got airborne with full afterburner, put the undercarriage up, and immediately pulled her up into a vertical climb, and carried out a roll-off-the top. The speed on top was 200 kmph! It was delightful to have so much power at your command.

The aircraft stalled in the most conventional manner, with the nose dropping down at stall, just like a slow speed trainer aircraft, with an easy, comfortable recovery. Most high-performance fighters are not even permitted to carry out a full stall, as there is always a danger of getting into an uncontrollable spin. But the MiG 29 was more docile than even a Kiran MK II in the stall. It is a great tribute to its designers, and a great boon to the pilots. As far as its low speed performance is concerned, I was able to carry out a loop in dry power starting at just 400 kph with hardly any buffet and perfect control. I also tried some really tight turns reaching 9 g which was the g limit given. Just to challenge my own physical fitness, I carried out a complete 360 deg. turn at a constant 8.0 g at 750 kph, with full afterburner, and without blacking out. Though I was at my body's limit, the aircraft was joyfully flexing its muscles. Even in tight turns at normal cruise power (without afterburner) there was hardly any buffet, and very little drop in speed. The aircraft, thus, had not only excellent power for its weight, but also super lift-to-drag ratio, giving excellent performance, along with great ease of handling – truly fulfilling the deep aspirations of any fighter pilot.

I also did one supersonic acceleration up to 1.7 Mach at 40,000 ft in full afterburner, and found it sailing through smoothly, with good control feel. There was not a murmur from the engine; obviously the air intake was doing its job pretty well. I then carried out an acceleration check at a low altitude from 350 kph to 1000 kmph, and found the aircraft running away from me, with my back pressed hard against the seat.

I carried out one formation flight along with another aircraft, which acted as my target, to check the radar interception capability at low altitude. The target aircraft flew at 2,000ft above ground, and I flew well above him at 8,000ft. First, the target positioned himself some 100 km ahead of me, and then turned around, for me to make a head-on attack in the ' look-down' mode, where my radar antenna had to point downwards to detect the target. Normally, when the radar antenna points downwards, there is a strong reflection from the ground, and the radar screen gets cluttered, making it impossible to detect the relatively feeble reflection from the target. But in the MiG 29, with the use of latest technology, the ground reflections were eliminated, and the target echo could be seen clearly in the screen.

I was able to 'lock- on' at about 60km range, and carried out a mock missile attack, without physically seeing the target. Thereafter, I closed in and sighted the target at 10-15km range, and followed through with a gun attack, using the thermal imaging system and the Helmet mounted sight. In this mode, the radar is switched off to prevent the target from getting any warning of the approach of the attacker. As the term suggests, thermal detection is accomplished by sensing the heat emitted by the target aircraft's engines. I could successfully carry out the gun attack without any problem, on this very first attempt. Undoubtedly the MiG 29 is a fantastic fighter, and flying it was a great treat. Such pilot-friendly design, and such superb performance.God bless the Russian designers and engineers.

Mirage 2000

In the mid 1980's, the Light Combat Aircraft (LCA) design activity was in full swing. As the CTP, I was also part of the design team, and was designated as Project Director (Flight Operations). Since the LCA was to be a fly-by-wire aircraft, I suggested that I be given some flying experience on the Mirage 2000, which had such controls; I could then give more meaningful inputs to the design team. A request was put up to the IAF, and they authorised me to fly the aircraft at the IAF base at Gwalior, which had two Mirage squadrons located there. I was to fly with No.1 Squadron, which was my old squadron – where I had flown the Vampire at Palam, and then the Mystere at Kalaikunda. And now, they had the Mirage. Some happy coincidence for me. I landed up at Airforce station Gwalior eagerly waiting to fly this beauty of a Fighter.

I carried out the ground training on the aircraft for a few days, learning all about the aircraft's systems, cockpit drills and emergency procedures. This was followed by a few dual flights, and then the first solo. Thereafter, I was left to do what I wanted with the aircraft!

The Mirage 2000 is a Delta wing aircraft with a fairly conventional cockpit, normal control stick and rudder, and foot brakes. Nose wheel steering was through rudder pedals. It had the usual systems common to high-speed fighter aircraft – Ejection seat, engine afterburner, variable geometry air intake, a Nav- Attack system and Head- up display like the Jaguar. The real novelty of the aircraft was, of course, the fly-by-wire flight control system. In this system, pilot's inputs through the control stick and rudder, are not connected in any physical way to the control surfaces on the aircraft. They are, instead, routed electronically to a high-speed computer, which acts as a mastermind. It analyses the pilot inputs against all relevant flight parameters and aircraft limits, and commands the hydraulic actuators to move the control surfaces accordingly. The aircraft's response is, thus, the optimum that the pilot can get under the flight conditions prevailing. In the earlier, purely mechanical or hydraulically powered flight control systems, the pilot had to pay a great deal of attention to ensure that while trying to squeeze the best performance out of the aircraft in combat manoeuvres, he does not exceed the aircraft's limits, such as max 'g' and max angle of attack. With a fly-by-wire system, the computer takes over this function, and performs it to a much higher level of accuracy and safety. This relieves the pilot of a heavy responsibility, with no fear of exceeding the aircraft's limits, and getting into trouble. What a great relief, this! Aptly, this feature is termed 'care free handling'.

With the intelligence and power of the high-speed computer, and high-speed control surface actuators, there is yet another profound advantage that the designers have been able to offer to the fighter pilots. They have made the aircraft very *agile*. The term 'agility' in this context is defined as 'rate of change of manoeuvre state'. In simple words, the faster you can alter the aircraft's flight path (from say, a tight turn to the left, to a similar tight turn to the right), the greater is the agility. And the higher the agility, the better placed the pilot is to out-manoeuvre the enemy fighter in a dog fight. It is thus a crucial parameter, which can make a difference between life and death for the pilot in a combat situation; literally.

When we want to have higher agility, an important factor to be considered is the aircraft's inherent stability, which in fact, is a 'force' that works to *oppose* any change in the aircraft's attitude or flight path. Thus, an aircraft with high stability would lack in agility. Conversely, an aircraft with poor stability can achieve high levels of agility. The only problem with poor stability is that it creates serious controllability problems for the pilot. This is where the fly-by-wire flight control system scores. With its high-speed computer and control surface actuators, it can provide a stable *response* in an *unstable* aircraft. To achieve this, the control surfaces need to move at a very high speed, under the watchful directions of the computer. Also, we need large and powerful control surfaces, so that they can provide large corrective forces swiftly to ensure stable behaviour. This is precisely what is provided in the Mirage 2000. It has very large moving surfaces along the trailing edges of both wings. These are called ELEVONS, so called because they provide the functions of the elevator as well as aileron. The left and right wing Elevons move in the same direction for pitch control, and in opposite directions for roll control. And since the aircraft was designed for poor longitudinal stability in order to enhance agility, the horizontal fixed tail surfaces, which provide stability, have been done away with. This aerodynamic configuration is called "Tailless Delta".

There is an automatic test facility in the aircraft to check the functioning of its complex Flight control system on the ground, prior to taxying out. After starting up the engine, the pilot activates the test by selecting a switch on the test panel, and waits for the Auto Test to commence. All control surfaces then spring into action, and move rapidly in accordance with a predetermined programme. During this period, the whole aircraft shakes vigorously, as if in severe turbulence, for some 30 seconds. Then, if all goes according to the programme, a green light comes on to indicate full serviceability of the system. The reason for the shakeup is the reaction to the rapid movement of the large control surfaces one way and another, the way it would need to operate in the air to ensure stable behaviour of the aircraft.

I carried out a total of 12 flights on the Mirage 2000 within a week of my stay with the squadron – at times flying up to three flights a day. The aircraft had excellent acceleration and climb capability – a must for any good fighter aircraft. Its flight controls were just superb, and I felt totally at home from the very first flight.

The aircraft had a maximum speed of 750 knots at low altitude and a minimum speed of 100 knots in level flight. On one occasion, I pulled the aircraft into a steep climb and throttled back the engine to idle power, to see if its intelligent flight control system recovers the aircraft without any inputs from me. I even took my hand off the stick. As the speed dropped to 100 knots, the aircraft started pitching down on its own to recover, and we touched a minimum speed of 55 knots in the process, a totally faultless execution of a tricky manoeuvre.

I accelerated to limit Mach 2.2 at 40,000ft in level flight with full afterburner. Supersonic handling and aircraft response were excellent. With my pilot's 'g' suit, I could sustain constant 8.0 g in a tight 360-degree turn at lower altitudes. I carried out all aerobatic manoeuvres and found the control feel to be excellent. I was able to execute a low speed loop at just 220 Knots with full afterburner.

I tried the Auto pilot in all its modes, including Auto navigation and Auto ILS, and found it very smooth, accurate and pilot-friendly. In the approach and landing mode, there was a unique pictorial presentation on the Head Up Display, which enabled a steady approach path at the correct angle of descent, angle of attack, and steady speed. The pilot had to align the speed, angle of attack and acceleration indicators with the use of throttle and stick to maintain the desired flight path down to touch down – a bit like a computer game! We have the same system on the LCA today and it works beautifully.

However, I found that the control *feel* during the approach and landing phase was not as good as I had expected, and it was not easy to promise a silky landing. Nevertheless, since the approach path guidance on the Head-Up Display was excellent, an average landing was assured. At the end of the day, I had to take my hat off to the designers of the aircraft for giving the fighter pilot so much of what he loves.

I returned to Bangalore on completion of my exposure to the Mirage, with a great sense of satisfaction, and a good understanding of this latest frontline fighter aircraft; one of the best in the world at that time.

xxxxx

In late 1987, I was appointed Executive Director for Flight Operations in HAL, which was a post at the HAL corporate office in Bangalore while continuing to be the Chief Test Pilot of HAL Bangalore. This appointment gave me the added responsibility of supervising flight test activity at HAL Kanpur and HAL Nasik as well. I was to monitor product quality relating to flight performance standards. I could choose to fly any aircraft in the three flying wings of HAL, and intervene where necessary, to ensure product quality. It was a mandate entirely after my heart. I would periodically visit Kanpur and Nasik Divisions of HAL, and carry out test flights on aircraft there, and have deep and rewarding discussions on various technical matters relating to recurrent problems on their aircraft.

Bombers

Canberra

At HAL Bangalore we had a few different versions of the Canberra bomber coming up for overhaul: the B-2, the T-4 trainer and the B-58, the last being the backbone of the bomber force of IAF. There were numerous differences between these versions in respect of their engines and systems, as well as their cockpit layouts. The B-58 was probably the best version with a fighter aircraft like bubble canopy, giving a much better outside view. Each version also carried a navigator, who had a cosy seat with a desk, at the rear of the pilot's seat. The B-2 and B-58 versions had a single pilot station, while the T-4, being a trainer, had two side-by-side seats and dual controls.

The overall performance and handling characteristics of the different versions of Canberra were, more or less of the same order. Thus, there was a common flight test schedule to be followed.

The Canberra was the first JET bomber of the IAF, acquired in the early 1950's from UK, and was quite a celebrated machine. Prior to this, we had a lumbering 4 piston-engine bomber of WWII vintage, called Liberator. These were also overhauled at HAL Bangalore prior to my arrival, but had been phased out since.

The Canberra was a medium bomber of British design with two Avon Jet engines, which gave it abundant power and excellent performance. It also carried plenty of internal fuel to give it a good attacking range. It could comfortably climb up to 50,000 ft and also attain its limit speed of 450 Knots in level flight at low altitudes. Its contemporary jet fighter, the Vampire, also had a similar limit speed, but attainable only in a dive. In this respect, the Canberra was superior to the Vampire! It also had a large bomb bay inside its belly, which could carry a heavy bomb load. The bay had doors, which when closed, could fully hide the bombs, thus eliminating any additional aerodynamic drag.

As I said, it had two powerful jet engines, one on each side on the wings. While these provided for excellent performance, they also caused controllability problems, if one of the engines failed when at maximum power; such as during take-off. In such a case, because of the asymmetry in thrust, the aircraft would yaw viciously towards the dead engine side. To control it, the pilot would need to apply full opposite rudder with tremendous force, straining the leg to the maximum, a condition no pilot could sustain for long. As a result, our drill in case of an engine failure at full throttle, was to throttle back the live engine a bit till the aircraft comes under easier control. This aspect of the aircraft had led to accidents on some occasions, but the benefits of higher engine power in military operations, was too precious to be diluted, so it was accepted.

The aircraft had a 4 'g' limit, which was adequate for a big machine like this. The flight controls were manually operated, but were well harmonized and comfortable. The cockpit had conventional instruments and was quite spacious, particularly on the B58. It also had ejection seats for the aircrew. All in all, it was an excellent medium bomber, and played a stellar role in bombing operations during the 1965 and 1971 wars against Pakistan.

Hindustan Aeronautics Ltd Bangalore
Part II

Transport Aircraft, Helicopters, NAL's Long EZ & Hang Gliders

C-119 Packet

The C-119 Packet, was a large Cargo aircraft used by the IAF, which was being overhauled at HAL. This was a twin piston engine aircraft of US design, and was the second transport aircraft acquired by the IAF after the DC-3 Dakota. It was a good work horse, with large rear opening doors for ease of loading heavy cargo. It had a much better performance than the DC-3. The IAF used it extensively for supply dropping operations in J and K and Ladakh, as well as for para jumping training for army troops. Since supply dropping at J and K and Ladakh involved flying at much higher altitudes, the aircraft's engine power needed to be enhanced. For this, HAL had installed an additional small jet engine on top of its front fuselage. This engine could be started in the air, when needed by the pilot, and switched off when not required. It provided for the much needed additional power at high altitudes, and enhanced safety of operations.

I found the Packet to be quite a nice aircraft for its role. Its flight controls were manual, but fairly light for its size, and made the aircraft easy to handle. It had an amazingly spacious cockpit with very comfortable seats and smooth engine controls. It had large transparent panels around the cockpit, giving a superb outside view. I have not come across such a grand cockpit design on any other transport aircraft of that vintage.

DO-228 DORNIER

In September '89, two new test pilots from IAF had come on deputation to HAL Kanpur. These two test pilots had not flown the Dornier 228 twin-engine commuter aircraft, which was being produced under license at HAL Kanpur. The Chairman HAL asked me to proceed to Kanpur, and familiarise the two pilots with the aircraft, to enable them to undertake test flights on it. I told the Chairman that I had not yet flown the DO-228 either! He merely smiled and said that I could manage it. I was not entirely happy to convert the pilots on an aircraft which I had not flown and knew nothing about, but I loved the challenge and landed up at HAL Kanpur,

I spent the next two days studying the Flight manual and learning up all about the aircraft. The two test pilots had already been through the manuals and were in a position to discuss the same with me in detail. I also spent some time in the cockpit along with the pilots to go through various drills and emergency procedures. Once that was done, it was time for me to do my first solo! I took one of the pilots to act as my co-pilot and carried out my first solo on it! It was an easy aircraft to fly, and I had no problem carrying out the flight: take off, climb, stalls, switching off and restarting engines in the air. The aircraft systems too were simple enough. Only, the engine was a pretty sophisticated turbo prop, and needed some special attention. I carried out a few touch-and-go landings and ended the flight, quite happy. After that, I did one more flight to get enough familiarity to be able to give them dual checks. Thereafter, I took the two pilots up, turn by turn, and let them fly from the captain's seat, self-acting as co-pilot and instructor. After a few dual flights each, the pilots were cleared for undertaking test flights on their own. I was happy to have managed it quite successfully. Sometimes, some tasks look much more difficult than they actually are !!

Airbus A 320 Crash Investigation

In 1989, a major accident to an Airbus 320 aircraft of Indian Airlines took place at HAL airfield in Bangalore. The aircraft crashed just short of the runway when it was on an approach for landing. It caught fire after the crash which claimed many lives, though some were saved.

I was appointed as a member of a 3-member accident investigation committee ordered by Director General of Civil Aviation. Detailed technical analysis revealed that under certain conditions, the auto pilot (AP) system could cause some ambiguity regarding pilot action. On the recommendation of the team, some changes were subsequently made to the AP system to overcome the problem.

While the inadequacy in the AP system could have confused the pilot a bit, by itself it could in no way have caused the accident, if only the pilots had exercised even a rudimentary level of *situational* awareness. The A 320 aircraft also had a voice alarm system (recorded in the black box) which had warned the pilot "You are too low, too low," and later "You are sinking, sinking," again and again, but the pilot did not respond, and stalled onto the ground.

The point then is, why did the pilot not respond? All he had to do was to cut off the AP by pressing a button on the stick, and open throttle and take full manual control of the aircraft. Here, the pilot appears to have been in a peculiar state of the mind, where it is entirely fixated on one particular aspect of the situation, which keeps him totally unaware of anything else, as if he is mesmerized. It is an extreme case of lack of situational awareness. Though it is a rare phenomenon, sadly, it does show up from time to time in aircraft accidents.

Helicopters

As Chief Test Pilot at HAL Bangalore, I had to exercise supervision in respect of Helicopter test flying as well. In order to do justice to this responsibility, I needed some hands-on experience on Helicopter test flying. My only experience had been flying the Bell G2 and G3 piston engine helicopters briefly at Kanpur, quite some years earlier and really had to start from scratch. We had a very experienced Helicopter test pilot called Chhoker, who had retired from the IAF as Group Captain, and joined HAL on a permanent basis. He was my instructor on Helicopters, and enabled me to eventually undertake production test flights on Chetak and Cheetah helicopters produced at HAL Bangalore. Chhoker (or Chokes, as he was called) was a real gentleman – always calm and cool, with gentle manners and a friendly personality. He carried out the first flight as well as much of the development flying of the Advanced Light Helicopter (ALH). He was a superb flyer and a great asset to HAL.

The Helicopter is a fantastic invention. Though it is, as a rule, a low speed, non-aerobatic machine, its aerodynamics is complex, and one needs to put in a lot of effort to attain proficiency in flying it intelligently. The method of piloting a helicopter is quite different from that of a fixed wing aircraft. This is primarily because it derives lift to get airborne, not by moving forward and creating 'wind' over the lifting surfaces, but creates lift while stationary by rotating its 'wings' – i.e. the rotor on top. There is a lever called 'collective' on the left side of the pilot, which controls the angle of the rotor blades. Pulling this lever up increases the angle of attack of the blades, thus creating greater lift for getting airborne. And pushing it down reduces the angle as well as the lift, which is what the pilot does for descending and landing. The first thing the pilot has to learn is to hover, that is take off vertically, and hold the helicopter steady at a height of say 10 feet. From there, to move forward, he needs to operate another control called "cyclic", which is similar to the control stick of a fixed wing aircraft, and is held and operated with the right hand. Moving the cyclic forward causes the rotor plane to "tilt" forward, thus creating a forward component of lift, which causes forward movement. Similarly, moving the cyclic back or to left or right causes the rotor plane to tilt accordingly, causing the helicopter to move backwards or sideways to left or right. What fantastic manoeuvrability!

Since the rotor has to bear the entire weight of the helicopter, it does so by pushing the air downwards to generate the required lift – just like the propeller of a piston engine aircraft needs to push the air backwards to generate forward thrust. Except that the mass, and hence the momentum, of the air pushed downwards by the rotor of the helicopter is very large, since the lift it generates must exceed the weight to enable a vertical take-off. This requires a very large rotational effort, called torque, on the part of the gear-box which drives the rotor. As a reaction to this torque, the entire body of the helicopter, would rotate in the opposite direction to the rotor. To check this unwanted rotation, another small rotor is provided at the tail end, which rotates in the vertical plane, and generates a side force to left or right at the tail to counter this torque effect. This tail rotor is controlled by the pilot's rudder pedals. To attain a steady hover, the pilot needs to continuously make fine movements of all the three controls – quite an arduous task. But to be able to hold the machine dead steady in a hover is a great feeling. Similar to formation flying in fighter aircraft .

One interesting exercise on the helicopter was to carry out an *auto-rotation*, which means to land with a failed engine; what is also referred to as a forced landing. In case of an engine failure in a fixed-wing aircraft like a fighter, the pilot needs to glide, that is descend, in order to maintain a certain minimum speed. It is like rolling down a slope in a car with the engine switched off. Of course, since he is continuously losing height ,he has to choose an airfield or a suitable landing ground urgently to force land before he loses all his height, or of course decide to eject! In a helicopter also, he is forced to descend if he loses the engine. But here, his primary aim is to maintain a certain *rotor speed,* since that is what gives him lift to sustain flight. For this, he needs to descend rather steeply in a dive to keep the rotor wind milling, and hence needs to choose a landing spot close by on which he can land. Thereafter, when he is close to touching down on the ground, he has to swiftly and drastically reduce his descent rate to get a safe landing. For this, he raises the COLLECTIVE lever rapidly to get the required lift to arrest the rapid descent. And, as he comes up on the COLLECTIVE, the rotor speed drops down quickly, turning it limp, and he loses control of the machine !! Thus, though the helicopter needs very little space for landing, the real challenge is not so much to find a suitable landing spot, but to judge the right moment when to pull up the COLLECTIVE lever. A little too early and you drop down like a brick, and a little too late, you thump down real hard. In both cases you are in for a shock !! It requires skill and practice to judge it right.

For a high speed fighter pilot like me, the ability to take off and land vertically, was too tempting to be confined to a helipad. Often, after completing the test schedule part, I would proceed to look for some beauty spots in the countryside: a lonely hill, a small clearing in lush green woods, or a quiet inviting patch of a half dried-up pond, and carry out a few landings and take offs there. In all of this, I enjoyed the beauty of the land enormously – something which seldom gets noticed in detail, if you are whizzing past at high speed. Appreciating beauty needs time, and flying a helicopter offers abundance of it!

DEVON

On one occasion, I took a Devon aircraft for a test flight. Though I found it generally satisfactory, I felt an unusual jerk on the aircraft from time to time. It felt as if one of its piston engines was missing a beat. I tried to check which of the two engines was giving this problem, but could not recreate it, in spite of manipulating all the engine controls repeatedly. After I landed I suggested that the engine ignition systems of both the engines be checked thoroughly, but nothing was really found amiss. The spark plugs were changed and tightened, and the electrical wiring was inspected to ensure all connections were secure. The aircraft came up for another flight the next day, and again I experienced the same jerks. The technical staff grounded the aircraft for a few weeks and checked the whole aircraft for any loose joints or foreign matter, or any other items not secured properly.

The aircraft came up for flight after the prolonged grounding with the hope that now the problem would not occur.

When I carry out external checks on an aircraft prior to getting into the cockpit, I have a habit of banging various parts of the aircraft with my fist as I go around it, just to check that there are no loose items left inside by mistake, during aircraft manufacture or assembly. This would show up by the vibrations I was imparting. I also give a mild kick to the nose wheel of the aircraft, where possible, for the same reason. When I did that on this aircraft, I heard an unexpected vibration from the rear of the aircraft. I asked one of the technicians to go back to the rear and try to locate the source of vibration, while I continued kicking the nose wheel! He found that the vibration came from the elevator. I cancelled the flight and asked them to remove the elevator and locate the precise source. When this was done, it was revealed that one bearing on the elevator had worn out badly, and somehow had gone undetected. Once this was set right, the problem was solved.

The lesson to be learned was that simple common sense is indispensible for any inquiry. However, one needs to remember that kicking won't always solve a problem, it may even create one, depending on where it lands! The kick, that is!

NAL's Long EZ

In February 1990, NAL (National Aerospace Laboratories), Bangalore had assembled a light piston engine aircraft called Rutan-Long EZ, using the drawings and kits bought from Rutan Aircraft Factory, USA. As NAL did not have a test pilot, they requested me to carry out its first flight. It was the first time that NAL had built an aircraft, so it was a historic moment for them. They had planned to have the aircraft for carrying out some flight research, and had in fact, formed a special department for it.

The Long EZ was quite an unusual aircraft, made entirely of composite materials (no metal)and hence very light, with superb finish to reduce drag. It had a small piston engine located at the *rear* with a pusher propeller. Instead of a tail plane, it had a *fore-* plane located ahead of the cockpit, with two small elevators on either side of the nose for pitch control. For roll control, it had the usual ailerons at the trailing edges of the wings. For yaw control, however, it had a novel arrangement of two separate rudders. Each *wing tip* carried a small vertical fin for directional stability, and each of these fins had a rudder at its rear edge. When the pilot applied force on the left pedal, the rudder on the left wing tip would deflect outwards and cause a yaw to left, the right rudder remaining neutral. Similarly to the right. However, if both left and right pedals were depressed at the same time, both rudder surfaces would deflect outwards, cancelling out the yaw effect, but increasing drag and providing the effect of airbrakes! Quite an ingenious design.

It was a two-seater machine with the two cockpits one behind the other. A single large canopy covered both the cockpits. The rear cockpit was meant for a passenger or baggage, and not really for flight training. The front cockpit had a reclining seat which gave the pilot a very comfortable posture for long flights. It had a small SIDE stick on the right-hand console, which had a relatively small range of movement for pitch and roll control. The undercarriage was very slim and delicate looking, the main wheels being provided with foot brakes. Funnily, while the main legs were fixed, the nose wheel leg could be retracted. For this purpose, the pilot had to crank a small handle under the instrument panel right in front of him, which would pull the leg up. Sometimes, just for fun, I would retract the nose wheel *before* getting airborne, when the nose wheel was raised off the runway but the main wheels were still on the ground. You could call it a low retraction! Just could not get over the obsession to do such tricks!

The aircraft had thick wing roots with extended chord, which had enormous inner volume for large integral fuel tanks. This gave phenomenal endurance for a light machine – some eight hours of flying time! The aircraft could, thus go on long cross country flights without stopping enroute to refuel. The reclining seat for the pilot was, therefore, a necessity.

I carried out the first flight of the aircraft in February 1990, amidst great jubilation in NAL. It opened a new chapter for in-flight research in NAL. Thereafter, I carried out all necessary flights to get the aircraft certified for experimental work. Once this was done, NAL would call me from time to time to undertake some test flights as per their requirement. I was, of course, still CTP at HAL Bangalore, but gladly accepted this additional task and enjoyed flying this aircraft – a welcome change from fighters.

Powered Hang Gliders

Sometime in 1989, when I was still CTP at HAL Bangalore, I got an invitation to witness some flying of powered hang gliders at the small airstrip at Indian Institute of Science, IISc, Bangalore. I had not seen this type of machine earlier, and was eager to have a look. It was to be during early morning hours, and I drove over in my Maruti 800 well in time. After a short wait, I heard a mild buzz overhead, and saw two powered hang gliders descending down in a spiral over the strip. They landed and I was introduced to the pilots – Joel Koechlin and Prof. Radhakrishnan. When I asked them if I could get a flight in their machine, they jumped at the thought, and said that they would heartily welcome me to join the circus, as it would also help in popularizing the sport. I was delighted at such a positive response, and so started my happy involvement with hang glider flying.

The first thing I noticed about the hang glider was that there were no separate control surfaces as such on the wing, and there was no tail! The entire wing had to be tilted this way and that to make the glider go where the pilot wanted it to. The wing itself was a combined pitch and roll control, and there was no yaw control! And the single control *stick* for this was a 4-feet horizontal bar rigidly attached to the wing and placed within easy grasp of the pilot, at about chest level. The body of the Hang glider was a light, tubular, metallic structure in the form of a tricycle, with the pilot's seat in front, and a stepped up second seat squeezingly behind it. At the back was the piston engine and it's *pusher* propeller; and lower down, below it, the fuel tank. The engine throttle control was at the pilot's right foot, much like in a car. There was a small, primitive instrument panel placed somewhat low and ahead of the pilot's knees, thus allowing a clear forward view. In fact, the front pilot had very little around him, and was right royally exposed to the elements. The wing itself was made of a special synthetic cloth, which was stretched tight on a light metal frame, and was strong enough to withstand the wind pressure. It was mounted on a universal joint to enable the pilot to tilt the wing forward, back and sideways. For directional control while taxying on ground, the pilot had to turn the nose wheel to left or right, by pushing the foot rests on the nose wheel to either side. And to fly it, all the pilot had to do was simply to push the control bar this way and that! Call it super multi-flexing!

I went up for my first flight in the rear seat, royally squeezed, with Radh flying from the front seat. He took off and climbed to 3,000 ft or so, and stabilized the glider in level flight at a speed of around 60 kph, and handed the control to me. I moved the control bar with both my hands gripping it, forward and back, and sideways gently, to get a feel of the machine and found that the glider's response to my inputs was rather sluggish, but it maintained level flight quite well, without much attention from the pilot. The only problem was that the sense of operation of the controls was exactly the opposite of what obtains on all fixed-wing machines, which is what I was so used to. Whereas in a fighter, when you pull the stick back the nose goes up and we climb, in the hang glider, when you pull the bar back, the nose would go down and we would descend. Similarly, if I want to turn left (or bank to left), on a fixed wing aircraft I would push the stick to the left. In the hang glider I have to push the bar horizontally to the *right* to tilt the wing to the left. So, I had to pause and deliberate before moving the bar in the required direction.

Because of my long experience of flying fixed wing aircraft, the sense of movement of controls on those machines had become a reflex response for me, as indeed it must. But now, I had to develop an *opposite* reflex to operate the hang glider! I thought it was a tall order!

However, with practice and concentration, I eventually reached a fairly proficient level, and felt cautiously comfortable flying the machine. So, I went ahead and did my first solo, and learnt first hand how the human brain could be tuned and re-tuned to suit the occasion.

Then followed many months of regular hang gliding, where I would drive over to IISc every morning by sunrise, and get aloft into the refreshing early morning air, getting more and more addicted to this simple, elemental way of spreading one's wings.

In February 1991, Joel Koechlin planned a hang glider rally – the route being: Bangalore – Mysore – Coimbatore –Dindigul – Tanjore – Pondicherry – Bangalore, with a few overnight halts. We took off on 22nd Feb, one after the other, and arrived at Mysore, landing on the golf course there. After a night halt, we took off early next morning for Coimbatore. I climbed up to 6,000 feet and settled down at cruise power, clocking around 75kmph, heading south for Coimbatore. The weather was fine and the hang glider was sailing beautifully, when all of a sudden I heard a sound as if something had hit the propeller, and it started vibrating wildly and then went limp. At the same time, the engine RPM shot up with an unnatural whine and the speed started washing off. I immediately cut the ignition to switch off the over-speeding engine, realizing that for some reason, the propeller had got disengaged from the engine.

I had no radio to call up and inform anybody about my predicament, and no choice but to force land the hang glider somewhere. But, when I looked down, I found that the entire terrain was undulating, with terraced patches of paddy, too small to attempt a forced landing on. We were gliding down at a speed of 60 kmph and losing height at a slow rate. The thought crossed my mind that if I just could not spot a clear patch, I would attempt crashing on to some tree-top to get as much cushioning as possible, and hopefully save my neck!

After some tense minutes, I spotted a dried- up river bed *far* ahead to the left. It looked too far to reach before I lost my height, but no harm in heading for it. Soon, we were closing-in towards the river bed, the last haven to safety, but at an excruciatingly slow pace, when I noticed that our descent rate had somehow reduced a bit, and we had more height in hand. As minutes and seconds ticked by, the possibility of being able to make it to the river bed also appeared to be more and more likely. As I came closer, I felt I had just enough height to make it, except that, now, I saw looming out of the haze, a gigantic stretch of high tension electric cables right across my approach path.

These cables were strung up pretty high between tall pylons and I did not think I could make it over them, and considered going under them – a treacherous proposition. As I was beginning to feel right royally trapped, a benign wave of gusts carried the hang glider aloft to a high enough perch to enable me to cross over the bank of cables – but just. I must have been no more than 20 to 30 feet above the deadly cables as I crossed over, and heaved a sigh of relief. I now saw that the patch of river bed ahead was covered with what looked like large stones, and I got a shock. But coming closer, I saw that though large, they were well- rounded, pebbles. Thank God for small mercies! I was able to make a reasonably good "rattling" touchdown, and came to a stop all in one piece.

When I examined the propeller, I found that one of its two wooden blades was badly chipped and broken, and the belt which drives it had jumped out of the pulley and was in shreds, totally disconnected from the engine. A closer examination revealed that a piece of bakelite bracket in front had cracked and flown off. It must have hit the propeller blade at the back, chipping it off badly and putting it out of balance and causing all the drama. It was a bizarre sequence of events, which had squeezed me into a tight spot, and virtually trapped me, at least for a while.

After I landed, the usual group of curious villagers swamped the place. I asked one smart looking youngster to guard the machine, while some others took me to the nearest telephone in a village by the name of Nanjangud. I rang up our emergency rescue number in Mysore, and got picked up in a van. The technical personnel took charge of the machine and transported it back to Mysore by road. I was taken by road to Coimbatore, where I joined the other pilots – all eager to learn what happened. I went through the rest of the rally on the rear seat of one of the other gliders.

I was disappointed at not being able to fly through the rally in my own hang glider, but in a way, happy that I got the experience of force-landing a hang glider. And anyway, all is well that ends well!

My Last Fighter Flight

The year 1992 was a watershed year in my flying career, as by end October that year, I would turn 58 and retire from HAL, bringing my military aircraft flying to an end. After that, no more fighters for me, and I would have to be content with light civil aircraft.

Somehow, of all the aircraft I have flown, the MiG 21 held a special place in my heart, and I eagerly awaited the moment for my last chance to fly it, which came a few days before I was to retire. I landed up at HAL Nasik on 22nd October to do the graces.

Early next morning, I am in the familiar Mig 21 cockpit and strapping up. I start the engine and welcome the familiar whine as it accelerates to idling RPM. A check of hydraulics, flight controls, air intake cone, jet nozzle, flaps and instruments indicate that all is well. I taxi out, check the brakes and roll down the taxiway towards the runway. The ease of ground handling gives the feel of riding a thoroughbred. Somehow, the pilot gets a sense of sturdiness and reliability in the MiG 21, which enhances his confidence in the machine.

There is no other air- traffic at that time, so I am cleared to line up on Runway 27, facing west. The wind is a gentle five knots and the windsock sways in a welcoming sort of way. I get an 'all clear' for takeoff, and open throttle gently to full dry power. After checking all engine parameters I push the throttle to full afterburner position and release the brakes. The afterburner lights up with a reassuring kick, and we shoot off down the runway. At about 350 kmph speed, I ease back on the stick and get airborne. I keep her low and retract the undercarriage. As I reach the end of the runway, I pull the stick back briskly to get into a steep climb, and then gently wing over towards the local flying area to the north-east. I lower the nose and accelerate to the climbing speed of 850 kmph, switching off the afterburner in the process. As we climb through two kilometre altitude, I flick the stick far to the left to execute a few crisp rolls, and rejoice at the prompt response. It is so easy to get the 'home again' feeling on the MiG 21.

I climb to 8 km altitude in 'dry' power and then cut in the afterburner to climb steeply to 13 km. As we approach a town called Dhulia, I turn around to right to head back towards the base, easing the nose down to level out at 13 km. Soon I cross Mach 1.0 in the turn, and we are supersonic. By the time I roll out on a south-westerly heading towards base, the aircraft accelerates to 1.3 Mach, and picks up speed at a good lick. At 1.8 Mach the air- intake cone position is an ideal 45 per cent and I can feel the air gushing through the intake channel with its characteristic impatient buzz. As we approach the limiting speed of 2.1 Mach, the aircraft starts skidding to left and right due to degrading of directional stability. I cut off the afterburner, and immediately the intake shutters open with a wild 'whoosh' that shakes the whole aircraft; a huge deceleration results. (Intake shutters on either side of the Air Intake are programmed to open automatically to permit the excess airflow to the engine to bleed off to atmosphere, as the engine cannot handle that much airflow with the afterburner switched off at high supersonic speeds). As the speed reduces below about 1.7 Mach, the shutters close shut, and things become calm again. Soon, we decelerate to subsonic regime and the aircraft controls feel much more responsive.

I descend below three km and carry out some aerobatics – loops, rolls, wing-overs etc. It is nice to feel the 'g' forces on the body – almost like a caress. It is surprising how an essentially uncomfortable force that pushes the pilot's body into the seat, temporarily increasing his weight many times over, can actually become enjoyable when the body gets trained for it by repeated exposure. Just as the long distance runner learns to enjoy his labours of exhaustion.

It was then time to carry out my favourite manoeuvre – vertical rolls. I dive the aircraft to 850 kmph, cut in the afterburner, and pull the stick back vigorously to get 6 g. As the nose comes up to the vertical position, a slight forward movement of the stick to check it there, and a large aileron input gets her to roll rapidly in a beautiful cork-screwing motion. As we complete 3 or 4 rolls and the speed drops to around 450 kmph, it is time to stop rolling and to pull back on the stick and get into the inverted position. Instead of rolling the aircraft on top to level flight, I keep pulling the stick back till the aircraft is pointing vertically downwards, and again start rolling.

Now comes the tricky part. In an aerobatic display, one must pull out by 500 ft above the ground. Here, you need to be extremely alert to judge the exact moment when the downward rolling must stop, and a brisk pull-out started. At that point, the aircraft is hurtling vertically down towards the ground at a speed of around 750 kmph. This translates into a descent rate of 700 feet per *second*. So, if you are 1 second late in starting the pull out, you could hit the ground. What is more, you cannot check your height by the altimeter, as it has a very large lagging error at such high rates of descent. Thus, you have no choice but to judge your height *visually*, by looking at the perspective of the ground, and start the pull out the *moment* you feel you *must*. Very much an animal response! The only way to develop such fine *judgement* is through repeated practice, starting at safer heights. Of course, one could play properly safe, and pull out at a higher height – but then the thrill and drama of the manoeuvre is lost. I chose 500 feet, and got it right every time, as my presence testifies! Sheer practice. Nevertheless, some onlookers told me that they felt scared that I might hit the ground. But, I have never doubted my instincts, and they never let me down.

After the adrenal pumping aerobatics, it was time to prepare for landing. I join circuit with 500 litres of fuel left, and peel off briskly to turn on to downwind leg, reducing speed and lowering undercarriage. I keep the aircraft a bit close to the runway, so I could carry out a steep curved approach. I roll out to align with the runway centre line at about 20 feet, and prepare for landing. As it was to be my very last flight on the MiG 21, I must admit to a pang as I touch gently down on the concrete and taxy back to the parking area and switch off; the nostalgic smell of hot brakes and burning rubber permeating the cockpit, as always.

I really felt sad bidding final farewell to a machine I had spent so much intimate time with, and so joyously. But all good things have to come to an end, sooner or later !!So be it.

Test Flying Light Aircraft

National Aerospace Laboratories (NAL), Bangalore

It was the month of October in 1992, when I was preparing to retire from HAL on attaining the age of 58 years, that I got a call from Prof. R.Narasimha, then Director of National Aerospace Laboratories (NAL) at Bangalore, and one of the most eminent scientists of the country. He said he had learnt that I was to retire from HAL shortly, and that he would like me to join NAL as Scientist Emeritus. I told him that I was a Test Pilot and not a scientist! He laughed and said it did not matter, and that he would appreciate my help with their aircraft projects. Of course, I had already been flying their Rutan aircraft. He also mentioned that it would not be a full-time job, and would be more on the lines of a consultancy. He said that there would be a modest stipend of Rs.4,000 p.m. from CSIR (Council for Scientific and Industrial Research). I told him I would be very happy to assist NAL and was least interested in any remuneration. However, he insisted that it would be proper for me to accept it as that was stipulated in CSIR rules. So I agreed, and thus joined NAL as Scientist Emeritus in Jan 1993.Over the next ten years, I would end up clocking over 500 hours of flying on their light aircraft projects with more exciting moments coming my way!

It was under the initiative of a senior scientist- cum-designer, Rustom Damania, that the very first aircraft called Rutan Long-Ez (Long Easy) had been built in NAL, using kits imported from USA. As I have already mentioned, I had carried out its first flight and a number of flights subsequently, to get its certification in the Experimental category. After that aircraft, Rustom with his team, undertook design of a two seat trainer aircraft to be made of composite materials developed at NAL. This aircraft, then called NALLA (NAL Light Aircraft), was slated to come out towards the end of 1993, and naturally I was to take it up on its first flight.

NALLA aircraft had two side by side seats, and a tricycle undercarriage. It was powered by a 100 H.P. Lycoming piston engine in front, which had a fixed pitch propeller. It had foot brakes but no nose wheel steer. Its manual flight controls were of conventional design. The cockpit was simple and quite comfortable. The canopy was in two independent left and right halves, which were hinged at the central strength member running above the pilots' heads, and opened upwards. After both the pilots got in from their sides, both halves had to be clamped down by ground crew, and locked in place by the pilots from inside.

I carried out the first flight of the aircraft on Nov17 1993, amidst much excitement in NAL. However, soon after getting airborne, I found the engine oil temperature shooting up menacingly and had to land back in a hurry. Obviously, the cooling air flow over the oil cooler was inadequate. This was rectified in a few days time by widening the cooling air intake, and we resumed our flights. In the next few flights, it became obvious that the aircraft was very under-powered, resulting in poor rate of climb. However, I continued with the flight tests to check out other aspects of the aircraft.

In one of these early flights, as I got airborne, the canopy on my side (i.e. the left half) opened up a few inches at the bottom front end. Possibly, one of the latches had not engaged properly. Immediately, a blast of air came gushing in, trying to pry it open further. I had to use a lot of force to hold it down with my left hand. At that time we were barely 50 feet above the ground and the extra drag due to the slightly open canopy did not permit the speed to go beyond 60 knots in level flight. This was only slightly above the stalling speed – an acutely uncomfortable situation to be in so close to the ground. The engine was at full power, resulting in a strong slip stream, which was only too eager to pull the canopy off my straining grip. Had that happened, I would have immediately stalled and, possibly, spun into the ground. Much as I would have liked to reduce power to soften the effect of the slipstream, I just could not afford it for fear of dropping my speed, and meeting a similar fate by another route! I had thus no choice but to doggedly hold the canopy down, straining my left arm to its limit, and land back as early as possible. But by then, we had already flown beyond the runway end, so I had to turn around and land in the opposite direction on the runway. It was really a 'touch and go' situation, as the speed was too low to execute a comfortable turn. I had to make it very very slow and shallow with just 5-10 deg. of bank to prevent the speed from dropping , and hoped like hell that I do not get into any turbulence or down gusts. It took ages to get the aircraft to turn around and point towards the runway, squeezing my patience and my left hand muscles to the limit. I had informed the Air Traffic Control about my predicament, and all other traffic had been held back to permit me to land. Finally, I did land safely, but not without losing a great deal of sweat and gaining a painful left hand!

In Dec.1993 the first air show in Bangalore, called AVIA INDIA, took place at Yelahanka airfield. NAL was very keen that their first designed aircraft should participate in the show. I had barely done some dozen flights on the aircraft, and it was really not ready for a display. But the occasion demanded that the aircraft should at least fly past there to showcase this major achievement of NAL. So I flew a few times, doing nothing but some gentle turns and showing off its lines. And of course, it got reported in the press, and NAL personnel were duly pleased. After all, it was their 'breakthrough' moment in aircraft design!

The aircraft was initially registered in the 'experimental' category and was, in due course, named 'Hansa'. I did numerous flights on it to check out its handling, and got more familiar with it. Since it was a non-aerobatic aircraft, there was not much one could do with it.

From safety point of view, the two critical tests were stalling and spinning. I carried out stall tests and found the aircraft behaviour quite classical. Recovery was easy and positive. After I had repeated stalls a number of times, I was ready for spin tests. Although aircraft of this class do not generally give any problem recovering from a spin, there is never a 100 per cent guarantee. All sorts of seemingly insignificant aspects of its aerodynamic shape have a major effect on recovery. And in case it does not recover, the pilot has no choice but to escape by baling out.

As a result, I had to get hold of a parachute from HAL –one where the pilot *sits* on the parachute placed on his seat. But the pilot's seat in Hansa was not designed for a seat type parachute, so I had to somehow squeeze it in, and sat on it in a cramped position, with my helmeted head almost touching the canopy. It was not the best way to go for spinning tests! I had tried to get a 'back' type parachute, but there were none of those available in HAL, or anywhere else in Bangalore at that time. So I just accepted the cramped position and went ahead with the spin tests. I carried out a few spins to left and right, and, luckily, found it to be perfectly normal, recovering every time within one turn. I was quite relieved that this tricky part of the tests was successful. After landing, when I got out of the cockpit, I had to execute a deep stretch to un-cramp my body!

By October 1995, NAL had procured a more powerful engine for the aircraft – an American Continental engine with 125 HP. I carried out its first flight on 17 Oct.1995 and found that the additional power made a big difference, making the aircraft more manoeuvrable and much better to handle. At a fly-in gathering of light aircraft at Jakkur airfield at Bangalore, I flew in a competitive display and bagged the first prize for a display on the aircraft.

I carried out numerous test flights on this aircraft to gather some data pertaining to design and various other aspects. It was then decided to obtain civil certification' for the aircraft under JAR-VLA regulations, a standard for very light aircraft(VLA). However, the aircraft was too heavy to qualify for this certification. So, a programme was launched to reduce its weight substantially to bring it within VLA standard. NAL engineers and designers got down to the task – the main aim being to reduce the weight of the aircraft *structure* itself. Many tests were carried out in the composite materials laboratory to see how the weight of the structure could be reduced without prejudice to its strength. With ingenuity and hard work, this task was successfully completed by the NAL scientists. A great job done.

As part of this weight reduction exercise, it was also planned to get a lighter engine for the aircraft. An engine named Rotax 914, with a horse power of 115 HP was chosen. Though the power was not as much as one would have liked, it was a lighter engine, and also had the advantage of a Turbocharger unit(TCU). This device ensures that engine power does not drop with increase in altitude, unlike normal engines, where the power drops progressively with increase in altitude due to drop in the air density. The turbo-charger on this engine was driven by the engine exhaust gases impinging on its turbine drive, and did not need any other power source. A truly economical device. The RPM of the turbocharger, and hence its output, was determined by the quantum of exhaust gases driving its turbine. This was electronically controlled by a gate valve. As the aircraft climbs up into thinner air, the gate valve opens progressively, to permit greater flow of exhaust gases on to the TCU turbine, which speeds up the TCU, causing more compressed air to feed the cylinders, thus compensating for the drop in the air mass flow into the cylinders due to reduced density . This restores the power to sea level value. Rather a long sequence but it works pretty well.

This aircraft with a lower weight and the new Rotax 914 engine came up for its first flight in Sept.1998. I found that the aircraft performance and handling qualities were much improved due to the lower weight. At 115HP with the benefit of a Turbo Charger, the power was quite adequate.

The Rotax 914 engine was unique in many ways. It was a high RPM piston engine, the max RPM being 5800, much above the 3000 RPM range of most other piston engines. This high RPM made it give a kind of humming sound - and not the normal staccato of the classical piston engine. It also had a variable pitch propeller, with a max RPM of 2350. Altogether, it was a very smooth running engine and very responsive to throttle movements. The Hansa, with the Rotax 914 engine became the final configuration for certification.

While, initially I was the only pilot in NAL, in due course we got one young civil pilot, called Yogendra Urs, to join us. He had no experience of test flying, but was well disciplined, keen to fly and got on well with everyone. Soon he became a useful member of the team. We did a lot of flying together on the Hansa and I was very happy to have his support and company. In April/May 1999, we took the aircraft to Pondicherry and Chennai for sea level hot weather trials, along with the ground support staff. In Chennai, I flew with a few flying club instructors to give them some experience on the aircraft, as they were slated to induct the Hansa into their club.

On 25 Sept 1999, back in Bangalore, the aircraft was prepared for its first-night flying test. The aim was to check the cockpit lighting as well as the adequacy of taxiing and landing lights, and of course, the general cockpit environment at night. I got airborne on a dark night and found the aircraft lighting quite satisfactory in most aspects, and noted a few improvements that were desirable. But by the time I finished the tests, the single radio on the aircraft packed up. I could, therefore, not contact the control tower for clearance to land. The procedure in such an eventuality was to fly past the control tower at a low altitude and flash the landing and navigation lights off and on to attract attention of the Air Traffic Controller and indicating radio failure. The control tower is then supposed to flash a green light signal, clearing me to land on priority. However, in spite of making a number of 'flashing' runs, I found no response from the control tower. I was in a bit of a fix, as landing on the runway at night without clearance from ATC was quite an unsafe option. Furthermore, there was some thunder and lightning close by and I had to land back soon to avoid getting caught in a storm at night. On the other hand, landing without clearance could result in a collision on the runway, if there happened to be some other traffic on it. It was a dilemma, and I was wondering what to do, when I noticed that a large transport aircraft with glaring lights was on short finals to land. It occurred to me that if I quietly sneak in immediately behind him, I would be safe from any other traffic on the runway, since Air traffic control would not clear any other aircraft to enter the runway till the landing aircraft cleared it. So, I landed 300 metres or so behind him to avoid his wake, and managed to clear off on to NAL's taxi track even before the landing aircraft could reach the end of the runway. A happy ending to a hazardous situation.

The next day I went to the control tower and asked them why they did not respond to my low runs with lights flashing. They did not have any answer but made profuse apologies. It is my guess that they were too busy having tea and chatting–such a common Indian habit- and were not keeping a sharp look- out as they were supposed to. When dealing with aircraft movements, such a lapse could have been dangerous.

In February 2001, an air race for light aircraft was organized from Bangalore, in which some eight to 10 aircraft were to participate. The route was pretty long, with numerous stops and two night halts on the way. The participating aircraft were to fly one after the other at the max. permitted continuous engine power specific to that aircraft. Each leg was to be timed visually by ground observers placed at each way- point, which all aircraft had to overfly. This would be compared against the best timing that particular aircraft was capable of at the stipulated engine setting. And, whichever aircraft got maximum percentage points, would win. It was not a race in the popular sense, but really a test of navigation accuracy. The more accurately you navigated, the greater was the possibility of winning the race. Thus, the slowest aircraft had the same chance of winning as the fastest!

I got airborne with Yogi on the morning of 4th Feb 2001, and set course for the first leg heading north- west towards Bellary. We climbed up to our cruising altitude of 8,000 feet, levelled off, and settled down at our cruising speed. All was going well, and we were on track. Soon after we passed the town of Tumkur, I sensed a slight vibration in the aircraft, which seemed a bit unusual. I thought it might be some mild turbulence in the air. But it appeared to be too regular for it to be turbulence. I checked my engine parameters and found everything within limits. After a while, I noticed that our speed too had reduced a bit.

This, of course, happens sometimes due to down currents in the atmosphere. So, I waited for some more time to check if it recovered to the original value. But, to my dismay, I found that the speed continued to drop further, though very slowly. The vibrations persisted without let up, but were within the broad spectrum experienced by pilots from time to time. I could have waited for some more time to see if a more visible problem showed up. But I had a hunch that there was some hidden problem of a serious nature, and so decided to abandon the rally and go back to the nearest airfield, and land as early as possible. I contacted Bangalore Radar and told them about my problem and requested to be guided to the nearest field for an emergency landing. The Radar guided me towards Jakkur airfield on the outskirts of Bangalore. I reduced power and setup a shallow descent. When we came within sight of Jakkur, we were at around 3,000ft altitude. I knew that I could not afford to increase power for fear of aggravating the engine problem. I also realized that at the existing descent rate, we would just make the field, aiming for the nearest runway end on the western edge of the field. I kept a little extra speed just in case the engine failed when we were slap over the buildings on our path. We arrived a bit high over the airfield boundary and I touched down quite a bit down the runway, possibly with some tail wind. I had some problem slowing down and stopping by the runway end, but just managed it. I taxied back to the parking apron and switched off. In a short while the technical staff from NAL arrived in a jeep and I told them about my undefined problem. After the engine cooled down, they opened the cowling and first, took out the spark plugs to see if there was any problem there.

They found clear signs of overheating on some of the spark plugs, but they could not figure out the reason for it. Anyway, the aircraft was taken back to NAL by road the next day, and a deeper investigation was set up.

While they were busy examining the engine in detail, I thought of checking if there was any problem with the flow of cooling air to the engine. When I checked the engine cowling (i.e. bonnet), which had been removed, I noticed that the cooling air channel on it looked rather narrow compared to other Hansa aircraft. Just to be sure, I went and checked the same on other Hansa aircraft in the hangar, and found that indeed, the channels on all other aircraft were much wider. It transpired that in order to improve the looks of the aircraft prior to the rally, the engine cowling had been re-shaped a bit, towards which end the cooling air channel on the inside of the cowling, had been made narrower. This was done without discussing its implications with the concerned experts. I discovered that this channel was aimed directly at the electronic ignition module situated right on top of the engine. I consulted the electronic experts if inadequate cooling of the ignition module could cause any problem. They were clear that it would *retard* the ignition timing. This would mean poorer combustion in the cylinders, leading to reduction in engine power and some over-heating. This matched with the reduction in speed, which I experienced, as well as the over-heating of the spark plugs observed later. Maybe some cylinders lost more power than others, causing the vibrations that I felt.

Now, in an engine with a fixed pitch propeller, any reduction in power would reflect as a drop in RPM. But on a *variable* pitch propeller, as on the Rotax engine, the propeller Governor would immediately make the propeller pitch finer, and restore the RPM. The pilot would thus find nothing abnormal in the engine parameters as reflected by the instruments. Yet, a power loss would be evident, if he was attentive enough. Precisely what I had experienced.

In this instance, just to make the aircraft aesthetically more appealing, a serious problem was unwittingly created on the engine. The lesson to be learnt was that in a machine, outer form is much less important than what is going on inside – a principle equally applicable to human beings!

My Very Last Flight

On 28th November 2002, I was completing precisely 50 years of active flying, and had decided to call it a day. It was on this very day, 28th November 1952, that I had done my first solo as a young Flight Cadet on the Tiger Moth in Begumpet, Secunderabad. I thought it was a good rounded landmark to end my flying career on.

On the occasion, NAL had organised a small farewell gathering of my colleagues and well-wishers, and I was to carry out the very last flight of my career on the Hansa, to be witnessed by them. I was happy that my wife, son, daughter-in-law and my two little grandsons were also present on the occasion. My daughter and her family were living in the US and, sadly, could not make it.

Test Flying Light Aircraft

When you bring to a close a neat 50 years of some activity that you have been deeply and lovingly engaged in, it is bound to be an emotional moment. I had to tell myself to keep my attention fully on the job at hand and not get carried away by the moment. I could not afford a mistake in this last flight of my career. So I took my own time, and kept my mind on the job.

I started the aircraft, and taxied out to the runway and took off into the clear morning sky, just like I had done thousands of times before. But the feeling was different – with the shadow of a profound parting looming over me. I climbed to around 2,000ft over the display area and carried out steep turns and wing-overs, and generally showed off the graceful lines of the aircraft against the sky (The aircraft was not designed for aerobatics). I flew for some 15 minutes or so, and finally came for the last low run over the crowd. As I passed the crowd and pulled up, I could not resist doing one last unauthorised roll, just to leave my signature in the sky. After that, I turned on to finals and landed and taxied back to the hangar, and switched off. As I hopped out of the aircraft, I threw up my cap as a final farewell gesture, and felt a pang. I had to steel myself before facing the applauding crowd. There were greetings and bouquets from my good friends and colleagues, who had always supported me so magnanimously. My youngest grandson, all of 3 years, came running up to me and said, "*Thatha*, you came so low and '*FLIED*' upside down". I picked him up and hugged him, little knowing then that in a few years time he would go far away from us all, into an enchanted fairyland. Such is life, a cocktail of joys and sorrows.

So came to an end my flying career of 50 wonderful years. It was a sad parting, but I had no regrets, as it was my own well-considered decision. I still felt quite competent to continue flying, and would have still enjoyed it, but I had made a resolve that the moment I saw any kind of decline in my performance in the air, I would quit. While I had not quite reached that point, there were some hints of it. I noticed that my ability to pay quick attention to a number of things at the same time, was declining. Having been in total command in the air for so long, I did not wish to lower the flag before quitting.

During my flying career, I had inevitably come through many ups and downs – many successes to rejoice in, and at the same time, several errors and narrow misses to reflect upon. I always felt that some unseen hand was protecting me at those crucial moments, when disaster could have been just inches away. It is impossible for any human being to ensure a correct decision within a fraction of a second, so one banks on appropriate reflexes. Somehow, these came at the right moments without my conscious participation. At other times, some dangerous situations just melted away, and kept me on a safe trajectory. I have experienced this on many occasions, and cannot but conclude that some benign hand was at work to give that little saving touch in the nick of time. I am forever grateful for the graces I so unfailingly received, and also for the warmth and understanding of all my colleagues who helped me complete my 50 years of flying on a happy note. And so, I say good bye, and God Bless !

My Brother Wg. Cdr. P. Gautam, MVC and bar, VM

My elder brother Gautam, was born in July 1933, and I followed 15 months later in October 1934. We were together for most part of our childhood and boyhood which was spent in Indore where our parents had settled. We shared an ayah who regularly took us out in a single pram. When we grew up, we climbed trees, had common friends, played marbles and tops together, and went for long pre-dawn runs. There was always a sense of togetherness between us, which never diminished even with the passage of time.

For some reason, we did not attend a proper school and instead, a tutor would come home and teach us. Eventually, in 1946, we both joined high school. Later, Gautam joined college in 1948 and soon applied for and was selected as an IAF cadet for 3rd course at NDA Dehradun in Jan1950.

I followed him a few months later and joined 4th course. As luck would have it, here too we were placed in the same barrack.

Both of us used to feel pretty homesick, and would often spend evenings together. On Sundays, we would take a walk to our favourite spot at the foot of a wooded hill, with a sparkling stream flowing nearby. It was a beautiful place where we were alone with nature, and an enhanced sense of togetherness prevailed.

Gautam graduated from NDA in Jan 1952 and joined the IAF Academy Begumpet, Secunderabad. I followed him six months later. On completion of flying training, Gautam got his wings and commission in April 1953, and I in January 1954. Thereafter our paths separated, Gautam joining the Canberra fleet and I ending up as Test Pilot.

Gautam took part in the Indo Pak wars of 1965 and 1971. He carried out daring bombing raids deep into Pakistan with spectacular success, and was awarded the Mahavir Chakra twice, once in each war. He was one of the highest decorated pilots of the IAF.

After the 1971 Indo-Pak war, he was posted to IAF Station Pune, as Chief Operations Officer, where he had to supervise all flying activity. Air force station Pune housed some Canberra bomber squadrons as well one MiG 21fighter squadron. Since he had not flown the supersonic MiG 21 till then, he was keen to do so. He immediately got down to complete the required ground training and soon started flying it, and enjoying it thoroughly.

Providence, however, has its own unfathomable ways, and on 25th November,1972when he took-off for his 13th flight, his engine failed immediately after getting airborne. As he was too low to eject, he had no choice but to force-land the aircraft in any open space he could find. Unfortunately, the terrain around Pune Airfield is very rocky and uneven and inspite of his best efforts, he could not avert a fatal crash.

I was stunned to get the news of his crash and was deeply shocked and pained. All my fond memories of our happy times together came rushing into my mind, and a deep numbness descended over me. I had to steel myself to be steadfast and strong for the sake of his family. It was the only way forward.

Though he was not much older than me, all through my early years, and later in the IAF, he would take me under his wing and guide me through my studies and career. As brothers, we had a unique relationship and a very special bond. We never ever had even an argument in our entire lives! There just wasn't any room for it.

The Family

Wg.Cdr. P. Ashoka comes from a family that is far removed from the world of flying aeroplanes. His paternal grandfather Sri Neelakantha Sastry was a civil engineer, Sanskrit scholar and a Theosophist, living and working in Tamil Nadu. He and his wife Smt. Seshammal, Wg. Cdr. Ashoka's grandmother, had eight children, four boys and four girls. Many of Wg. Cdr. Ashoka's uncles and aunts distinguished themselves in their chosen fields and were closely associated with the Theosophical Society. His eldest uncle, Sri N. Sri Ram, was a journalist and philosopher who became President of the Theosophical Society headquartered in Adyar, Madras. His aunt Dr. N. Sivakamu was a highly regarded surgeon and family physician to the maharaja of Bikaner. Another aunt, Smt. Rukmini Devi Arundale, was a well-known bharatanatyam dancer, founder of the dance school Kalakshetra in Madras, and nominee for President of India. Others had eminent careers in education and science.

Ashoka was born in 1934, the second of four brothers. His father Sri N. Padmanabhan was a physics professor who worked in Calcutta, Lahore and Indore and retired as Principal of Holkar College in Indore, Madhya Pradesh. His mother Smt. Maitreyi Padmanabhan was a student of Maria Montessori and a passionate Montessorian. She worked for about five decades in Indore, teaching in, directing and founding several schools. Wg. Cdr. Ashoka's older brother Wg. Cdr.P.Gautam was a pilot in the Indian Air Force. His younger brother Professor P. Krishna was a physics professor at Banaras Hindu University and later, Rector of Krishnamurti Foundation India in Rajghat, Varanasi. His youngest brother, Wg.Cdr. P. Ajit was also a well regarded Test Pilot with the IAF.

Wg. Cdr. Ashoka and his wife Meera live in Bangalore enjoying a retired life. They have a daughter and son and three grandchildren.

Vrinda Ashoka

Daughter

Author

Wg Cdr P Ashoka was born in Indore, MP in 1934. He joined National Defence Academy, Dehradun, in 1950 and after 2 years there, joined Air force Academy in Begumpet, Secunderabad in 1952 for Flying training. He was commissioned as Pilot Officer in Jan 1954, and posted to a Fighter Squadron. From 1954 to 1962, he served in various Fighter Squadrons of the IAF. In early 1963, he was selected for a Test Pilot's course in the prestigious Empire Test Pilots' School at Farnborough, UK, where he graduated with flying colours, winning two trophies at the graduation ceremony. On return to India in 1964, he was posted at Air force Station, Kanpur as a test pilot, where he stayed for four years. From 1968 to 1992, he worked with Hindustan Aeronautics as a test pilot, initially on deputation, and later got absorbed as a full time test pilot. He was the Chief Test Pilot at HAL Kanpur from 1968 to 1975, then at HAL, Nasik from 1975 to 1983, and finally at HAL, Bangalore from 1983 to 1992. At HAL, Bangalore he also held the post of Executive Director, Flight Operations, at HAL Corporate Office from 1987 to 1992, in addition to being the Chief Test Pilot there. On retirement from HAL in October 1992, he was invited to join National Aerospace Laboratories at Bangalore as Scientist Emeritus and Test Pilot, till he ended his flying career in October 2002 at the age of 68 years.

His passion, daring and drive during his 4 decades in the challenging field of test flying, earned him many commendations and awards, and bestowed upon him the status of a legend. Now, at 84 years of age, Wg Cdr Ashoka leads a retired life with his wife, Meera, at Bangalore. Their daughter Vrinda and son Dileep are both married and settled, and are in regular touch.